Rom .

MW00440062

The Blooming of a Daisy

Surviving the Storms of Life Through Faith

Dee B. Price
(Daisy)

Written in 2007 by

Dee B. Price
AKA: Daisy Belle Kelley

Dee B. Price
"Daisy"

The Blooming of a Daisy: Surviving the Storms of Life Through Faith

Published by WheatmarkTM
610 East Delano Street, Suite 104, Tucson, Arizona 85705 U.S.A.
www.wheatmark.com

ISBN: 978-1-58736-891-2
LCCN: 2007930382

DEDICATED TO:

My three precious children:
Duke Lamont (Monty), Gina Lynn, and Terri Sue
*Clark   ****   Beck   ****   Daugherty*

ALSO

To my grandchildren:
David Alexander and Douglas Lamont Clark
Lyndsay Marie and Summer Dawn Beck
And all great grandchildren!

INTRODUCTION

Many have lived in poverty and it is always a painful journey. Rejection hurts and healing is slow. This book is focused on four aspects of loss, difficult experiences, and recovery. The near abduction interrupted by a sister's cry for help is one section of the book. The huge flood that destroyed our home and led to moving to a shanty makes up another episode.

The transition from Indiana to Arizona alone at the age of seventeen was a difficult move, especially since I knew no one in Arizona. The last straw was having my life savings of $60 stolen from me as soon as I arrived here. The survival after that was amazing.

The story tells repeatedly of God's love and protection, of His unwavering care and the endless supply of grace and mercy bestowed upon me. Yes, this book is about surviving, overcoming and learning to go forward. Abraham Lincoln said: "I may walk slowly, but I never walk backwards." That was me, plodding ever ahead, seeking what was before me. Philippians 3:13 – "Brethern, I count not myself to have apprehended; but this one thing

I do, forgetting those things which are behind, and reaching forth unto those things which are before." KJV.

The blame game is prevalent in our society. I believe we are accountable for our own faults and failures, realizing all have sinned and have fallen short of His glory. We cannot go back and place blame on the fact of deprivation in our childhood. We must learn to lean on our Lord through the good and the bad times of our lives. He is always faithful, not wanting harm to come to any. I am thankful for my life, just that I have this awesome journey. I am thankful that He has come into my life and is my personal Savior. He has given me His perfect provision. Hallelujah – What a Savior!

ACKNOWLEDGEMENTS

I THANK GOD FOR always being by my side, for pre-vailing over the evil one, and for any talent he has given me for writing. May it always glorify Him. I thank Him for the times He said NO to me when it would have proven not to work for my good.

THANKS TO DUKE (MONTY), GINA AND TERRI – My wonderful children, for their loyalty in always standing by me in every situation. I am thankful for any and all family members who have in any way inspired me to put this book together. I thank Steve and Terri for helping me with the technical fine points. Gina has helped me with advice since she has published three books. Monty has been a constant inspiration, never doubting my ability to do this.

I THANK BECKY STERTZBACH – My patient editor who was willing to give me encouragement and help where I needed correction. Becky is an editor with the International Baptist College in Tempe, AZ. I feel so fortunate to have found her to assist me.

ELLEN LUCAS – I give thanks to my special friend – a real Barnabas to me. Her insistent encouragement to write the book spurred me to do this. I appreciate her faith in me and her love for me.

THANKS TO MY MANY FRIENDS who have come alongside when I really needed them and have been a source of rich encouragement.

TO MY SISTERS AND BROTHERS who have been uplifting to me – I give thanks.

TO DAVID S. PRICE – My dear husband who has had to bear with me as I took the time to write this book. One thing about the computer, you can always turn it off and save the works until you have another minute. David has been inspiring and helpful to me in this project.

A SPECIAL THANKS TO LORI SELLSTROM of Wheatmark who stuck with me to the last detail of this book. I do so appreciate her comments, patience and insight in helping me to get it all right.

CONTENTS

CHAPTER 1

....

A Shot in the Dark

Psalm 116:6 "The Lord protects those of childlike faith; I was facing death, and he saved me." NLT

Psalm 121:2-3 – "My help cometh from the Lord, which made heaven and earth, He will not suffer thy foot to be moved; he that keepeth thee will not slumber." KJV

THE TEARING OF THE window screen fit into Daisy's dream. She did not realize it was for real. The dark figure at the window was about to get the screen off and pull Daisy out the window. It was on a hot July night and Daisy had put her pillow in the window sill which was right next to her bed. She thought she could catch a breeze that way. There was no electricity and therefore no fans in the house. The family dog was barking away at the man. That, too, became a part of Daisy's dream. Just as the man was about to grab Daisy, her sister, Henrietta, woke up and saw the man. She screamed, "Daddy, Daddy, someone is getting Daisy." With that, Dad Kelley sprang out of bed, in his long underwear, grabbed his .32 pistol, and opened the front door. He fired two shots in the man's direction. The dark man ran down over the embankment in front of the house out into the black of night, never to be seen again. This all happened when the family lived in the shanty, or "shack" as Mom Kelley called it. Daisy was then about 9 years old. ("God Will Take Care of You" – Civilla D. Martin, 1869-1948). Surely, surely, Daisy's help had come from the Lord, the one who watched even in the darkness of the night.

Although no one actually slept the rest of the night, Daisy was so frightened that she was allowed to sleep between her parents the rest of the night. No one had ever been allowed to do that before. Henrietta had saved Daisy's life! God would reward her in heaven for that. God has a purpose for every thing and Daisy did not yet know about this one. ("In Times Like These, you need a Savior…My anchor holds and grips the Solid Rock…"- Ruth Caye Jones - 1902). Daisy loved the old hymns and they cover just about every situation – especially her relationship with Jesus Christ. What a wonderful path – the path of old hymns.

The Lord had spared Daisy from this awful fate. There must be a reason that she was not aware of at the time. God has his purpose in everything. Why did this man come to this house, this room, this window, for this girl? The two shots in the dark were so convincing that those questions did not get answered. In her childlike faith, Daisy knew her help did indeed come from the Lord.

There were lots of thankful moments then. Daisy had a protective father, strong and quick to act. The evil one did not prevail. Her sister awakened at just the right time. Praise God from whom all blessings flow abundantly.

Just living in the shanty had its challenges. The lack of plumbing, electricity, or even the bare necessities of life, made it rather bleak. It was always "make do." There must have been something better coming, the family hoped. The Lord would make a way.

> *Psalm 16:7,11 "I will bless the Lord, who hath given me counsel; my reins also instruct me in the night seasons." "Thou wilt shew me the path of life; in thy presence is fullness of joy; at thy right hand there are pleasures for evermore." KJV.*

CHAPTER 2

Mud Center –
In the Beginning

Luke 18:16 But Jesus called them unto him, and said, "Suffer little children to come unto me, and forbid them not: for of such is the kingdom of God." KJV

DAISY WAS BORN IN Evansville, Indiana, in a neighborhood dubbed Mud Center. It was really Pleasant Center but when it rained, and that was often, it became a real muddy place and thus the name Mud Center. She was the third child born into the large Irish family of William Henry and Lula Mae Kelley. Most of the children were born at home.

Webster's Dictionary describes a daisy as a ray flower, even a weed in some parts of the United States; but the next definition is nicer. It describes "Daisy" as a first rate person. Yet another description of "Daisy" is "Eye of the Day." Isaiah 40:31. *"They that wait upon the Lord shall renew their strength, they shall mount up with wings as eagles..." KJV.* That was a lot to live up to and Daisy knew she would be a weed some of the time, but she liked Phil. 4:8 regarding that thought. Daisy knew that all that she was, or ever hoped to be would be through her Lord and Savior.

By the time Daisy was three years old, she had the whooping cough along with her sister Henrietta and brother Leroy. Daisy was the smallest, youngest and the most vulnerable for lasting lung damage. She later developed bronchial problems relating to that. There were no medications at that time for the whooping cough. Mom Kelley lined her children up each day for a dose of cod liver oil whether they needed it or not. Daisy's parents were not bent to calling doctors.

The house in which Daisy and her family lived in there in Mud Center was very adequate by today's standards. They had a basement where the furnace was housed. They had a phone, electricity too. There was no indoor plumbing however. Dad Kelley had built a playhouse out in the backyard. It was a large one. When storms came Mom Kelley would gather her family and head for the playhouse. She felt it was safer than the house ("A Shelter in the Time of Storms." – Vernon J. Charlesworth - 1938). Many times neighbors came and gathered in there too. It was large enough to accommodate them.

In the first grades Daisy, along with the other kids, walked to White School. There was a corner to turn about a block away and most days, when

Daisy got to that corner, her mother would call her back. "Daisy, come back here." Daisy would go back and her mother would say: "Don't put your foot on the pavement. A car will come and run over you. And don't get in the car with a stranger. You will be dragged off to your death." Sometimes Mom Kelley would call Daisy back twice before she could get around that corner. There was no way Daisy would fail to obey either of the two admonitions. It proved that repetition was effective. She never forgot those two warnings. ("Wonderful Words of Life" – Philip P. Bliss – 1838-1876). God always watched over her during her childhood.

At school Daisy was a favorite of the janitor and the principal. They liked little Daisy and made her feel so special. One of them would lift her up so that she could be the one to ring the school bell. They thought of her as "A Daisy 'Belle' Ringer." What power Daisy felt as she watched the children scramble to get to their rooms. One day it was so cold, her feet felt just frozen. A kindly teacher wrapped her feet in newspapers and put her by the heaters until she was warm. That was another teacher to be thanked and God would reward her. The principal and the janitor loved Daisy's long brown curls which her mother carefully coifed each morning. They told her they wanted one when they were cut.

In the first grade, a time came for all the children to get shots. Daisy's parents had signed the papers for her to get the immunization shot. Daisy hid under her desk. All the children left the class to get the shot. In a short while two huge eighth grade boys came and found Daisy hunched under the desk. The boys took each of Daisy's arms, and they hauled her off to the nurse. No escape was possible. Daisy shrieked in pain as the nurse administered the shot.

Later, the children went to West Heights School. When Daisy was in the fifth grade, her father came to the school. He was very angry at one of the teachers. He entered the classroom and threw his hat which landed in the wastebasket. He was upset because one of the teachers had scratched Leroy, Daisy's brother, on the neck in a basketball game. It seemed the scratch was deep and went untreated. Nevertheless, Daisy was totally embarrassed by the incident. Dad Kelley ranted at the teacher and they had him leave for disturbing the class.

The little country church (General Baptist) was just across the street from Daisy's house. The children went regularly, but Dad Kelley seldom went. Mom Kelley loved to go when she could. Daisy's Mom and her sister, Henrietta, used to dress her up in pretty pink fluffy dresses for church and Sunday School. Daisy loved to go. The minister, the Reverend Wayne Snodgrass, had a monkey. The monkey sat on his shoulder a lot. One day the monkey was in a bad mood and bit the tip of his ear off. They never saw the monkey much after that.

Reverend Snodgrass had a wife named Cora. Years later, a younger sister named Cora was born to the Kelley family. A brother was given a second name of Wayne. The church was a big part of the Kelley family's life. Mom Kelley was secretary to the Ladies' Aid Society in the church and they sometimes met in the Kelley home.

Christmas at the church was very special. At the end of the service, they gave each child a bag of candy. They loved that. Usually, the children recited poems they had memorized. Once though, Daisy was scheduled to be on the program and had memorized "The Night Before Christmas." Since the family had no car, they were dependent on other people to pick them up. Mr. Light always picked them up for church. The night of the program came, but Mr. Light did not show up. The children wanted so badly to go to the program. They watched at the window for the lights of his car, but he did not come. Mom Kelley told the children to go to bed and forget it as it was obvious he was not coming. That was such s disappointment to the children. They cried as they went to sleep. Daisy lived in Mud Center until she was 8 years old. That is when life started on a slippery slope for the family.

If I Could Go Back Home

If I could go back to that house I once had,
Where I lived in our "home" with my Mother and Dad,
I'm sure I'd appreciate it more than I did then.
We had a passion for living through the thick and the thin.

I'd like to be listening to my mother's advice;
I'd hearken to her wisdom – wouldn't that be nice.
I never heard my mother pray but I know she did.
She asked God to watch over me when I was a kid.

We can't go back or change any of the past;
Needless to say, all the good things would last.
We can have a new start and do unto others,
And be a real blessing to our sisters and brothers.

But the years pass by and we can only think back,
To the times when we lived in the house or shack,
The house still stands, but the heart is not there,
The good part about it is that we all still care.

We won't be regretful about our place back home,
Though most of us have let our minds roam,
To the house we once knew in another time
Tomorrow is here, the time is prime!

—Dee

Isaiah 43:18,19 (NIV) "Forget the former things; do not dwell on the past. See, I am doing a new thing! Now it springs up; do you not perceive it? I am making a way in the desert and streams in the wasteland."

CHAPTER 3

Grandma Brown

Psalm 71:18 "Now also when I am old and gray-headed, O God, forsake me not; until I have shewed thy strength unto this generation, and thy power to every one that is to come." KJV

EACH SUMMER, ONE CHILD at a time was allowed to go to Grandma Brown's house for two weeks. What a joy that was to them. Daisy would pick cherries off a tree in front of the house and Grandma would make cherry dumplings. Grandma (Lear) and Grandpa lived out in the country. She was the paternal grandmother. She was married to Grandpa William Kelley until he died. She then married Edward Brown. She had only one child and that was William Henry Kelley, Daisy's father, born on July 18, 1887. The children did not know much about their father's background.

Grandma always had such good vittles including home baked yeast bread, pickled beets, Kentucky Wonder green beans, and rhubarb sauce. When the food truck came around to Grandma's house, the children were allowed to pick out something from the truck. When Daisy was visiting, she always picked Philadelphia Cream Cheese. It cost 17 cents. Little did Daisy know then that Grandma only got $5 to last the whole month. Grandma never let on that it was any hardship. God would reward Grandma many times over for her kindness and generosity. Grandma loved the Lord and served Him faithfully. She was a great example to all.

Before she was saved, she used to put a little snuff on the inside of her bottom lip. The children never saw much of that as she had quit by the time they spent much time with her. She loved to play checkers and the kids all loved to play with her. She always won.

Sleeping at Grandma's was such fun for Daisy. She slept in a great big feather bed and sank low into it. A big Grandfather Clock stood in the room. It was a pendulum clock and it went tick-tock every hour.

Some Sundays, the Kelley family all descended on Grandma's house. She always loved it and had great meals for them. In her living room she always had a large quilt frame up and a quilt in the making. She made so many beautiful quilts. When Daisy was about 12 years old, Grandma gave her the blocks she had made of a Baby Doll Quilt. Daisy treasured that quilt.

Grandma knew how to pick "greens." She

could pick them anywhere and knew which were good. She and Step-Grandpa went fishing in a nearby creek. They would pack a lunch and set out for the day. They usually carried home enough fish for supper to go with the "greens." There were times when Grandma would ask Daisy to dust the old Singer sewing machine, some odd tables, and other furniture she no longer could reach. Daisy thought it nice to do this for Grandma.

Grandma's only son, W. H. Kelley, had been married before when he married Daisy's mother. They had four children, daughter Sophia and sons McKenzie, Leonard, and Clifford. The first Mrs. Kelley died when Sophia was 12 years old. She was the oldest of the four. Sophia would come to their house and make snow cream. Mom Kelley used to say to never make snow cream from the first snow as it would be unclean.

William Henry Kelley married Lula Mae Ryon sometime around 1920 or 1921. Both parents were born in Kentucky. Together they had ten children, Daisy being number three in the lineup. Henrietta was first, then Leroy, Daisy and then Tom. Barney and Odell came along then, and after them Melvin, Cora, Margaret and Paul. It seemed to Daisy that her mother was pregnant all the time. She was pregnant a total of seven-and-a-half years. There simply was no way Dad Kelley could support this family decently. Mother was shy, submissive, and uncomplaining.

The Kelley children never knew their maternal grandparents. They lived in Kentucky. When Daisy was about 5 years old, she remembered her mother getting a phone call informing them that the grandmother had died. Her mother sank in a chair. Soon grandfather died too.

Grandma Brown always said: "Reputation is what people say you are – character is what you really are." Grandma always told Daisy to say to Grandpa Brown: "Grandpa Brown, went up town, with his hat upside down." Grandma Brown was one to listen to. She was wise in many ways. The children loved her and had great respect for her. She loved her Lord most of all and it did shine through to Daisy and her siblings. She went to meet her Lord in 1948. She had certainly shown her strength to the next generation. *Psalm 100:5 "For the Lord is good; his mercy is everlasting; and his truth endureth to all generations." KJV*

CHAPTER 4

....

Brother Tom's Accidents

Romans 12:10 & 12: "Be kindly affectioned one to another with brotherly love; in honour preferring one another." "Rejoicing in hope; patient in tribulation; continuing instant in prayer…" KJV

WATERMELON ON THE FRONT porch of the Kelley home was always a fun time. Sometimes neighbors would come and join in the fun. One evening while this was going on, younger brother Tom, went to the back yard and climbed on top of a lumber pile. Dad Kelley kept lumber around for his job. Tom had fallen off the top of the pile and was on the ground only half conscious. He seemed Ok though. He was noted for being accident prone. Another time, he backed up into Mom Kelley's wash tub. She managed to pull him out quickly. He had an adventurous life it seemed. Mom Kelley would need a lot of hope and patience for the tribulations to come.

It was Christmas and Dad Kelley had gone shopping for the children's toys. When he re-

14

turned, Mom Kelley discovered that he had forgotten Tom's gift. She insisted he take Tom and go back to get his gift. In so doing, Dad Kelley was not watching Tom and he fell into a manhole cutting his eyebrow badly. He took Tom home bleeding all over his little sailor coat. Mom Kelley, who seldom spoke up to her husband, said that he must take Tom to a doctor. Dad Kelley did that and Tom received about seven stitches. Tom was about five or six years old at the time.

Another time Dad Kelley took the family in the old Whippet to see a job he had just finished. It was a basement and everyone had to descend on a ladder. When the family was ready to leave, somehow Tom did not come back up the ladder and was left there in that basement. On the way home, Daisy was taking a nose count and noticed Tom was missing. She informed her parents who insisted that he must be in there somewhere, but he was not. Dad Kelley said he would take the family home and then go back to hunt for Tom. When the family got home, lo and behold, there was Tom riding a tricycle on the sidewalk in the back yard. When asked how he got there, he said a policeman had brought him there. It was incredible that a six-year-old could tell the policeman where he lived. It was surprising too, that the policeman had left him there alone.

Brother Tom had other accidents too, but these were the main ones. God watched over him and gave him His protection. Brother Tom was delivered so many times. – Praise the Lord!

> Philippians 1:19 "For I know that as you pray for me and as the Spirit of Jesus Christ helps me, this will all turn out for my deliverance." NLT.

....

CHAPTER 5

Traditions of Christmas –
One Gift

*2 Corinthians 9:14,15: "And in their prayers for you
their hearts will go out to you, because of the sur-
passing grace God has given you. Thanks be to God
for his indescribable gift!" NIV*

WHEN THE CHILDREN WERE small, and Christmas
came, they were warned not to wake up in the
night. If they did and happened to see Santa, they
would be given a bag of switches. None would
dare to open their eyes. Each child was given one
gift. The gift would be hidden and they had to hunt
for it. Traditions of Christmas at the Kelley's house
went this way:

'Twas the night before Christmas, when all at our house,
Were stirring, yes, even our mouse;
Our stockings were hung on the back of a chair,
No chimney for us, so we hung them there.
We went to church on Christmas Eve night,
And listened to the sermon and closed our lips tight.

We were told beforehand that we must be good,
As old Santa Claus by the doorway stood.
He gave us candy in a big brown sack,
On the way out the door, and a pat on the back.

Then home we went and off to bed.
We snuggled in tightly and covered our head.
Momma said that we must not peek,
So our eyes were tight shut, we were so meek.
For if we should look and see St. Nick
Lo, in the morning we would get just a stick.
When morning came we searched for our one gift,
Knowing for sure it would give us a lift.
Our one present, our parents always hid,
We didn't know where, but they always did.

When in a while, we found our one treasure,
We were delighted way beyond measure,
We opened our one gift as quick as a wink.
I always got a dolly; she was pretty in pink.
The brothers got a truck, car, or some toy,
It was always so much fun and brought us such joy!

Our stockings were stuffed with candy and fruit,
Whatever it was it would always suit.
We kids did not know that we were poor,
'Cause old Santa could always get in our door.
We said "Merry Christmas," we knew He reigned,
And you know what – no one complained.

Our thoughts wondered back to that Holy Night,
When Jesus was born, and made our world bright.
He was The One Gift, God gave to us all.
He came to save us – the great and the small.
Traditions, traditions, for Christmas, remain the same,
It's all about Jesus – Bless His Holy name.

By Daisy (Dee)

CHAPTER 6

....

Antics of Tom and Daisy

Proverbs 29:25 "The fear of man bringeth a snare: but whoso putteth his trust in the Lord shall be safe."
KJV

Tom and Daisy often went through train trestles. They had no way of knowing whether a train might come along. There was not room enough for people and a train. God was still watching out for them and kept them safe.

Tom and Daisy, along with other siblings, often would crawl inside a barrel and roll down a hill inside the thing. The hollow, as they called it, was a fun place with lots of trees. It was a rough ride and often times would hit a tree at the bottom for a final jolt. What a bumpy ride that was.

Daisy was a bit of a fun loving girl. One Halloween, the other children were all sitting on their bed looking at valentines they had received a while back. Daisy slid off the back side of the bed and went under the bed unnoticed by the others. She then began pushing up on the springs of the bed. The other kids were scared. They thought someone was about to get them. They called loudly for Dad Kelley. He promptly came with the .32 pistol and pointed it under the bed. Daisy was frantic. She called: "Daddy, it's me Daisy. Don't shoot me." She crawled out and he gave her one of those looks that Daisy knew well. "Just one look – that's all it took." This time Daisy knew she was a weed.

Henrietta and Daisy were walking home through the park, which was part of their back yard, so to speak, and they saw a man behind a large oak tree. He was beckoning to them to come by him. Upon closer inspection, they could see it was old man Ball (not his real name) from down the street. He was totally naked. The girls were so frightened that they immediately started running toward home. When they told Mom Kelley, she told them not to tell their Dad. She said he would kill Mr. Ball and then they would all suffer. There would be no food on their table. The girls just avoided Mr. Ball forever after. They just decided that he was not a nice man. This time Daisy was the "Eye of the Day."

Tom and Daisy would climb one of the big oak trees in the park. They would just sit up there and view their surroundings. Once they got a surprise. A young couple came along and sat right under the tree. What Daisy and Tom viewed was a real revelation!

The Kelley's had two pigs. Every time it rained, they routed out of their pen. Tom and Daisy had to go chase them down: those were Dad Kelley's orders. This was when they lived at the "shack." They ran barefoot – they never wore shoes in the summer time - through the hollow and over into another field. Daisy stepped on a broken bottle and nearly cut her big toe off. Finally, a neighbor helped them get the pigs back. When they returned to the house, her foot was bleeding profusely. Mom Kelley wrapped it up in some rags and it eventually healed back together. There was no mention of a doctor visit for stitches. God was Daisy's great physician, caretaker, her all in all. The children marveled at their survival of these incidents. Daisy had trusted the Lord but had no idea how often He would keep her and her siblings safe.

One of the neighbor's goats got out and came into their yard. It chased both Tom and Daisy around the clothesline pole several times. Mom Kelley came out with a broom and yelled at the goat. She grabbed Tom out of the circle and took him in the house and Daisy was still running around the prop. She came back and got Daisy then and shooed the goat away. Mom Kelley was brave when it involved the safety of her children.

CHAPTER 7

A Turning Point –
Precious Moments

Acts 16:31 "Believe on the Lord Jesus Christ, and thou shalt be saved…"KJV

DAISY AND HER FAMILY kept going to the little country church – a General Baptist Church. One night after a stimulating sermon, Mom Kelley urged her three oldest children to accept Christ into their hearts. Henrietta, Daisy, and Leroy all went forward to the small altar and knelt there to receive this wonderful blessing. They did not know much about the scriptures, much about the Apostle's Creed, or much of anything, except they did know they needed a Savior. Even though they did not know a lot, Daisy believed that God saved them unto Himself. Daisy knew she must not tell fibs, must be nicer to her siblings, and must always be obedient. Growth in knowledge would come with maturity. Daisy always held onto her faith. ("Amazing Grace, how sweet the sound, that saved a wretch like me." – John Newton – 1705-1807). She attended church wherever she was. That was what held her together. God did marvelous things in her life. She later rededicated her life. Wherever she was, the first thing she did was find a good Bible-believing church to attend. God was always there for her. ("When We Walk with the Lord, in the light of His word, What a glory He sheds on our way... and with all who will Trust and Obey." – John H. Sammis – 1846-1919). The glorious hymns of faith tell the whole story of salvation, the Christian walk, and of one's eternal destiny. This minister of the church spoke the real truth even about Hell. He not only told about Hell, he affirmed that it was a real place, eternal, and awful in the worst way. He read it right from the Holy Scriptures. Daisy would have to say a lot of prayers as she did not want even one of her loved ones to enter Hell. She was to have lots of encounters with her Lord in prayer later in life. (Justification.) Though Daisy was only a bud at this time, she would keep on blooming.

In the spring of the next year, Daisy, her brother Leroy and her sister Henrietta, were baptized in the cold waters of the Wabash River. The crowd sang "Shall We Gather at the River" – Robert Lowery - 1826-1899. First, there was a morning service at the church in New Harmony, Indiana, where Brother Snodgrass was the minister. Cora Snodgrass, his wife, insisted that Daisy come up and sing "Jewels, Precious Jewels, His loved and His own" – William O. Cushing -1823-1902. Singing was not one of Daisy's talents, but she did her best. Mrs. Snodgrass wanted Daisy to sing because Dad and Mom Kelley were in the pews. They had dinner on the church grounds and later all went to the River for the baptism. Being the shortest, and youngest, Daisy was left in shallower water with a deacon while the others were baptized. It was very meaningful and Dad and Mom Kelley were on the bank of the Wabash looking on. Daisy would never know what they were thinking since they never said. It was just a real pleasure that the parents came to witness the baptism.

Reverend Snodgrass and wife, had a son, Jack. He gave Daisy and her sister, Henrietta, their first and only ride in a rumble seat of a car. What a thrill that was for these girls!

When times were good, Mom and Dad Kelley would go shopping. They would bring home a dress for Henrietta and Daisy, a shirt or pants for the boys. They always brought home a sack of chocolate drops and orange slices. The orange slices became a favorite of Daisy's. They looked forward to these times of shopping. Sometimes Dad Kelley would bring home a large sack of cinnamon rolls. There were some good times then that the whole family enjoyed so much.

By the time Daisy was 8 years old, Dad Kelley had begun drinking alcohol more heavily. He would take the family with him to the store and on the way home, stop at a bar, leaving the family to sit and wait. One such time on the way home he fell asleep at the wheel at the edge of a cliff. Mom Kelley did not drive or know much about a car, but she stepped on the brakes and turned off the key just in time. She got out and took the children and walked the rest of the way home. It was about a mile and a half. The cliff was near the levee in Howell. She left him sleeping there over the wheel. When she got home, he had somehow gotten there with the groceries. There was no mention of the incident and no apologies were made. From then on, it was downhill financially. Dad Kelley kept up his drinking and though little was left owing on the nice home, he lost it. The family was devastated and had to move. They were on a slippery slope from here on for a time. ("Only Trust Him."- John H. Stockton –1813-1877) It seemed to Daisy that excessive alcohol drinking always led to a sad ending. The move went forward to an old hotel on Franklin Street. They had only two rooms on the second floor. Daisy could see the pride go out of her mother. The children had to enter a new school. Things did not go well there. At one point, Dad Kelley was cited for driving while intoxicated. His punishment was to spend 30 nights in jail. That was so that he could still work and support his large family in the daytime. He would go home and get a pillow and return to the jail. While he was in jail, the family had very little food. At one point, for nearly three days they were without food. Brother Leroy had three cents. He took it to the small grocery store nearby and told the owner the dilemma of his family. He stated that he had three cents and asked the man to please give him the most of anything he could get for his pennies. The owner of the store filled a brown paper bag with loose soda crackers. Leroy brought it home for them to eat. The family thought it tasted like steak. At other times Leroy would bring home ears of corn, or other vegetables and watermelon from the farm where he worked. It was always good and much appreciated. Leroy worked at a very young age.

While Dad Kelley was spending nights in jail, one night Daisy decided to crawl over to her mother's bed in the dark. She was a bit mischievous, a weed. Her mother thought she was a bull dog and kicked Daisy with her foot, sore from an ingrown toenail. Daisy then told her mother who she was and all was well. Later Daisy wondered why she would do such a foolish thing as to scare her mother.

Brother Leroy decided that Daisy needed a sex education class and he would be the teacher. On the way home from Pleasant Chapel, he stopped walking midway across the bridge. He told Daisy never to let a guy kiss her except in the way that he would show her. He pressed tight lips across hers ever so lightly, and said: "Now, if any guy kisses you any other way, you slap him." The boys in Daisy's time were so timid, they barely would hold a hand, much less kiss her. Thankfully, she never did need to slap anyone.

Mom Kelley had so many sayings. Daisy kept a list of them. She did not like black cats to cross her path. She always said the children should not be near animals or windows during lightning storms. She was extremely scared of storms and would ask Daisy and the other children to pray for safety during these storms. Needless to say, she did not go under ladders. She thought bubbles in your coffee cup meant one would have money. If anyone dropped a knife, a woman was coming, a fork, a man was coming, but to drop a spoon meant a fool was coming. Small raindrops meant hail was on the way. She used to say "There is more than one way to skin a cat." She had many of these different expressions. Daisy found herself repeating some of them.

....

CHAPTER 8

The 1937 Ohio River Flood

Jeremiah 17:7-8 "But blessed are those who trust in the Lord and have made the Lord their hope and confidence. They are like trees planted along a riverbank, with roots that reach deep into the water". NLT

THE FLOOD WAS EVANSVILLE's greatest natural disaster. Damage was everywhere. It started with an ice storm in January of 1937. Limbs breaking off trees with the weight of the ice sounded like gunshots. Days of rain and snow followed. The city was inundated. Typhoid shots were given in some cases. Sewers were full and overflowed into the streets. This was a horrible disaster. Newburgh became home to lots of cattle. Kentucky farmers brought them there on barges because Newburgh was higher ground. Everyone was singing "Lord lift me up and let me stand, By faith on heaven's tableland; A higher plane than I have found – Lord, plant my feet on higher ground." – Johnson Oatman, Jr. – 1856-1922.

Classes were canceled in most schools in the

area. Homes were destroyed including the Kelley's. Water had to be boiled for safety. Even through all of the distress, the power stayed on in Evansville. In 1913 there had been a flood of the Ohio River that reached 61 feet. But in this 1937 flood in Evansville, the river crested at around 55 feet. And in other towns such as Shawneetown, Illinois, the river rose to 66 feet. All of these facts were reported in the Evansville Courier and Press.

The book of Genesis tells the story of the big Flood. Noah had built an ark to be prepared for it. In Evansville, another flood came and the family had no ark. God does do marvelous things with a purpose. ("Keep Me Safe Till the Storm Passes By.") In sending that flood, the family would at least have to move from the old hotel. A man came knocking on the doors. He told Mom Kelley that she had fifteen minutes to get her family out and down the stairs. Mom Kelley was scared because her husband was at work. She grabbed all the children and headed down the stairs. The family was loaded into a big truck. The family dog, Blackie, was there and Leroy wanted to take him on the truck. The men said the dog could not go. Leroy responded that he would not go if they had to leave the dog behind. In their haste, the men shoved the dog on the truck and away they all went. At first, they were taken to a Red Cross Building. That building soon became full and all the people were hustled off to the Chrysler Building. When they arrived at this new shelter, the dog jumped out of the truck only to be picked up by the dog catchers who happened to be right there.

The families were given a little corner of the room with cots. The shelter had food to serve but Mom Kelley would not let her children have any as she had feared they would get lost in the crowd – and besides Dad Kelley would not like it. So the children and their mother all stayed very hungry. Dysentery was wide spread and Daisy got it. What a miserable night they spent there in that huge crowded building. It was a long night since no one could really sleep.

The next morning Dad Kelley found the family. He had tried to come home from work only to find their home flooded. The water had risen to the second floor. The old hotel building was condemned. Dad Kelley took the family to his mother's home in the country. He went to the dog pound and got the dog back. The family stayed at Grandma's house for two weeks waiting for the waters to recede. By this time there were six children in the family, so it was a handful for Grandma. All of this reminded Daisy of the old hymn: "God Leads Us Along." – G. A. Young – 19th Century. ("Some through the waters, some through the flood, Some through the fire, but all thru the blood, Some through great sorrow, but God gives a song, In the night season and all the day long.") What a comfort to know that He cares and gives the answers and comfort in the

night and all the day long. Grandma Brown was always a source of great joy to all her grandchildren.
She died in 1948, but did not go before she saw
Daisy's firstborn, a son. Her faith roots went deep
and she passed that on to the next generation.

CHAPTER 9

······························

The Shack

Hebrews 13:2 "Don't forget to show hospitality to strangers, for some who have done this have entertained angels without realizing it." NLT

SINCE THE FLOOD DESTROYED the old hotel, Dad Kelley had to scrounge up another place for the family to live. In the move, Mom Kelley and Daisy had taken the family cat and put it in a large bag. They cut a hole in the sack so the cat could breathe. They boarded a city bus with the cat which was really not allowed. They hoped against hope that the cat would not make a sound. It did, but it was not too noticeable and they were able to transport the cat to the new home.

This time, Dad Kelley rented an old place: Mom Kelley called it "the shack." This "house" had a kitchen, living room, one bedroom, and one small cot- sized room. Of course, no electricity or indoor plumbing was there either. The little shanty was dull. The first thing that brightened it up was a Christmas tree, the family's first one, which was left over from the school program. There were no lights or decorations to put on it. The children cut paper to string on it just for some color. This was no time to be just sitting on the premises It was time to be "Standing On The Promises that cannot fail." They were poor as church mice. They didn't know of any "Wheel of Fortune" coming their way. Eventually Dad Kelley did manage to build another house for the family to move into and then a final one after that. The last house he built was the best. By that time there were still nine children left at home. Henrietta had married and moved away.

Mom Kelley was a good cook. Her recipes were all in her head for she had no cookbook to go by. On Sundays she cooked chicken and dumplings. She made the best ones ever. Chili was another of her specialties. There would never be an evening meal on Sunday. Saturday there would be breakfast and an evening meal of beans but no lunch. No free lunch is one thing, but no lunch? Needless to say all the children liked the weekdays better because there was lunch at school. Supper was always beans of some variety. On special occasions, Mom Kelley would make Kelley hash. She made it the night before and it was for breakfast. She would cook a roast and add potatoes and onions the next morning. At breakfast they always had biscuits and Karo syrup. The many tummies could fill up on that. Mom Kelley made the best cobblers in town. There were never any leftovers to worry about. Dad Kelley said the blessing before every meal. It was so mumbled that what Daisy heard was "Bless the cigar foam." For years she watched men with cigars to see this foam and never did see any. After several years, thinking back, she realized that what he actually was saying was "Bless us in our home."

There must have been a time when Dad Kelley made a decision to follow Christ and ask the Lord to forgive his sins. There is reason to believe that he will be in heaven. He was baptized in the Ohio River: in fact, he had to be dunked twice since the first dunk did not get him all the way under. No Bible-believing minister, especially a Baptist, would baptize anyone unless they had made a profession of faith in Christ. Also, he spent a lot of time on his knees beside the bed. Who was he praying for? Was it Daisy, or would she be at least one of them? Could he have been praying for himself or for the family?

Dad Kelley allowed, even invited, people to come for cottage prayer meetings held by the church. They would come to this humble shack and gather around the bed or anywhere they could stand. They would sing, pray, and read scripture. Dad Kelley seemed to like that. Daisy never knew when or if her Dad quit drinking, but she thought he had in his later years, since he was able to build another house or two. Hope springs eternal.

One thing missing in Dad Kelley was encouragement for his children. He withheld that, and any outward show, or words, of love. Once in a while, when he came home from work sober, he would hold them one at a time on his lap for a minute. That was always precious to the children.

Dad Kelley was a good singer. He sat on the front porch a lot and sang "Can I Sleep in your Barn Tonight Mister? For it's cold lying out on the ground, and I have no place to lie down..." Sometimes he would sing "Red River Valley." That was one record they had that could be played on the old Victrola. It was Henrietta's job to crank it up and play their few records, like "The Daring Young Man On The Flying Trapeze."

Other times Henrietta and Daisy would rock in the wide rocker and sing all the old hymns they knew so well. They did not know that Dad Kelley was listening out on the front porch. Mom Kelley's favorite hymn was "In The Garden." (C. Austen Miles, 1868-1946). The girls sang that a lot for her.

Mom Kelley had an old rooster she called Old Jock. She loved this old guy and enjoyed watching him wander in the yard. She had to grab on to anything that was pleasant. By others standards, her life was considered drab and dull. The old rooster cheered her up. Another pleasure she loved was to go shopping, with Daisy, and then to a small restaurant where they could "tank up." They could get a bowl of chili, a hamburger, and a coke for fifteen cents. That was such a treat.

When hobos came to the door, Mom Kelley always made them a sandwich of something to eat. Dad Kelley thought that it should be that way and that no one should be turned away. Daisy could remember that many of them came to the Kelley door and even though they were poor, they always could find some food to share with the less fortunate. They showed real hospitality. Were these hobos some the "angels"?

Daisy thought it was incredible that none of the children in the Kelley family drank alcohol. Was it because they saw the misery it had brought to their home? Did they not like it? In any case, it was a real blessing in that household.

Dad Kelley smoked a pipe; sometimes even a corncob one. There was no thought in those days of second-hand smoke or the harm it could do to the lungs. The pipe had a good smell. No one was aware of the affects of the smoke at that time. Daisy knew later on that it was not good for her to breathe that smoke.

CHAPTER 10

Danger Zone

Philippians 4:4-7 "Rejoice in the Lord always. I will say it again; Rejoice!... Do not be anxious about anything, but in everything, by prayer and petition, with thanksgiving, present your requests to God. And the peace of God which transcends all understanding, will guard your hearts and your minds in Christ Jesus." NIV

TOM AND DAISY WERE very close growing up. They did everything together. They crawled through culverts that could have been very dangerous had water come through or if they had encountered snakes. God always watched over them in all their adventures. They walked across frozen lakes not knowing how thick the ice was. What a wonderful Savior they had then and still have. Another time a group of black boys surrounded them in the park. They scared the daylights out of them. They threatened to hurt them. Tom and Daisy were sorely outnumbered. All of a sudden, Daisy yelled out: "Tom, look, here comes our Dad." Of course

Dad Kelley was nowhere in sight. But the boys did not know that so they scattered and ran. Daisy and Tom ran the other direction and got away. Bluffing was always a good way out when a person is small. These kids were not hard to bluff. ("Rescue the perishing...Jesus is merciful, Jesus will save." – Fanny Crosby – 1820-1915). Praise the Lord again and again.

Some mornings, Tom and Daisy would have to ride a bike about 4 miles to get the day's groceries. Their hands would be so cold. It was a hard ride and they felt that no one cared.

Mom Kelley would get the children all scrubbed and dressed for church even in the shanty. One day Tom and Daisy were the first ones ready and went outside and stood at the top of the embankment. Suddenly Tom shoved Daisy over the hill and she rolled down the muddy path to the bottom Her dress was ruined. She came back to the top and pushed Tom down the same path! What a shock to look around and see Dad Kelley standing there. They were marched to the woodshed and Daisy got her licking with the belt first, and on her way to the house, she looked back and there was Tom getting his. That was one time when they felt they deserved what they got. Daisy was a weed again.

The Kelley household had strict rules – no card playing, no movies, no dancing, in fact, most any fun was a "no-no." The children could play "Old Maid" or checkers. They had to do homework by the light of a kerosene lamp. It was not a good light, but it was the best they had. ("Brighten The Corner Where You Are"). They still managed to get good grades in school.

The shanty was set at the base of Mesker's Park. There were large oak trees off to the west and Daisy remembers a persimmon tree. On the other side was a quince tree. No houses were very close to this place. It was at "the shack" where Daisy nearly lost her life when the dark man appeared at the window of her bedroom. Was it an accident that she was spared? Daisy never thought so. She believed that God woke Henrietta up to scream for her Dad. Obviously the man was intent on dragging Daisy out the window and to a terrible unknown fate. He was so close to getting her out. What a marvelous blessing that God intervened even in a terrible scene like was told at the beginning of this book. She was saved by His marvelous grace again.

Girl friends did not want to come to spend nights at Daisy's house because they could hear the lion's roar in the zoo. They thought that too scary to deal with. What if one got out?

Daisy finished up grade school at West Heights. While there she played softball on the team. She always made good grades. She played a clarinet in the band. Dad Kelley would not allow her to go out at night so she was not able to participate in the band then. The teacher even told Mr. Kelley that he would personally come and get her and bring her home. His answer was staunch – she was not allowed to go out at night. Mr. Brooks, the teacher, was saddened by that answer. When graduation time came, the students went on a trip to French Lick, Indiana. There was a cave they explored. Daisy wanted to bring home a souvenir but had no money. So she wadded up a ball of clay from the ground and took it home with her as a remembrance of the trip. Any trip for Daisy was rare.

There were times when Dad Kelley would play a game with the children. They loved that. There were not many times when there was a show of caring. He would play softball with the kids, but they did all the chasing and he did all the hitting. He did eventually get to where he would give each child a nickel a week. They thought that was great.

One Christmas the kids went shopping for their own gift. Each one had been given fifty cents. Daisy saw a toy clarinet she wanted but it cost fifty-one cents. Her brother, Tom, knew she wanted it badly, so he gave her one of his pennies to get it. Daisy would never forget his generosity. The one thing they had that cemented them together was love. There was so little love expressed or shown in the Kelley household. It seemed to be so difficult for their parents to express love.

Tom and Daisy were "put out" of the house each day in the summer months to fend for themselves. They would sit on the doorstep and dream about what they would do when they grew up. Both wanted to go out west. Tom wanted to be a cowboy, and Daisy wanted to work in a candy store. They did a lot of dreaming about what life could possibly be for them. But this growing up part was hard. At times when they were wandering through the park, they would find themselves looking at tables where people had been eating. They were hoping they would have left a morsel behind for these two hungry kids to find. Sometimes they would find a hot dog or a bun. Daisy and Tom stuck together through the few good times and many bad ones. It was after Daisy was eight years old, that all began to slip away. The family could all feel what was happening. The smile went out of Mom Kelley's face. The children were sure she thought about what could have been. It was sad to see her expression change.

Mom Kelley knew Dad Kelley would likely come home drunk. So she stationed the children at the windows to watch for him. If his pants and belt were below the waist line, they knew he was drunk; otherwise not. Most of the time, he was drunk. Mom Kelley feared what he might do in that case, so she often sent the children to bed with no supper. Daisy often wondered – why did her father drink so much? Was he depressed? It was soon after the big depression that he started drinking. He had worked hard in the cement business. He did work for WPA and the CCC camp. He had built "mountains" in the zoo for the animals to climb on, and his name was etched in the cement sidewalks around town. He had talent in that field and taught it to his sons. Usually, he was not wordy or mean when drinking. He seemed rather subdued and melancholy. Daisy's mother always told the children that drinking alcohol excessively would shorten a life and she believed it would do so with her husband. She was right. It did.

The lady playgrounds keeper at the Mesker Park liked Tom and Daisy. She became their friend. Nellie even took them to their first movie. She more or less watched over them knowing they were not being properly cared for at home. They loved Nellie and were so appreciative of her. Sometimes she would even buy them an ice cream cone or something. God put people in their paths like that.

CHAPTER 11

....

Aunt Daisy from Texas

Romans 8:28 "And we know that in all things God works for the good of those who love him, who have been called according to his purpose." NIV (Aunt Daisy's life verse.)

FORTUNATELY FOR THE KELLEY children, there was Aunt Daisy Belle Lininger. She sent letters with a dollar in it designated for one child each letter. The children always gave it back to their mother. Aunt Daisy prayed for the children, gave them help, and supplied their shoes and some clothing. The children would draw their foot on a paper and send it to her and she would send shoes to fit. She sent packages that contained candy and nuts, along with essentials. What a joy it was to get her packages. She was a wonderful aunt. She even sent Daisy her clarinet to play at school, albeit, it was outdated. The teacher loaned her one. Daisy loved playing the clarinet. Daisy had played softball too all through her school years.

"The command to 'trust in the Lord' is no half-hearted hope of a reluctant heart. On the contrary, it is a conscious acknowledgment of Him 'in all your ways.'" —*Charles R. Swindoll. Taken from Insight for Living 2003 calendar, "Adventuring With God." (Used by permission.)*

Daisy liked that especially the hope. Those days could be rather bleak and she needed that blessed hope that only He could give. (My Hope is built on nothing less, than Jesus blood and righteousness. – Edward Mote – 1797-1874).

Aunt Daisy kept in touch and was Daisy's encourager. She always had a scripture to offer and she sent reading material. Her sphere of influence was wide. What a wonderful servant of the Lord she was. Daisy was named for this aunt, thus her full name, Daisy Belle Kelley. Aunt Daisy was a listener, a helper, a saint of God and an angel of mercy sent into Daisy's life. Aunt Daisy was married to Charles Lininger and they had three sons, Jack, Bill and Gene. She lived in Electra, Texas for some time and then moved to Lubbock.

When Daisy was sixteen years old, she went to visit her Aunt Daisy. There she met her cousin Tom Williams. They liked each other right away. She noticed Aunt Daisy had lots of pills. She took them regularly and Daisy thought it foolish to take so many. But Aunt Daisy lived to be 95 years old, so there must have been something good in those pills. Uncle Charles gave Daisy pages of work to type for him and then paid her for doing it. Daisy thought everyone should have an Aunt Daisy. She continued to be a blessing to Daisy until she passed away.

Aunt Daisy was a tract lover. She bought bright colored cellophane paper to wrap them in. She called them Gospel Bombs. She threw them out over bridges into the rivers, in parks, and along the roads. She did get some responses. Once when Daisy was traveling with her, she asked Daisy to throw some out too. Sometimes the air was cold but Auntie would always say, "God will take care of his workers and not let them catch cold." This was her ministry – spreading the Word! The Fanny Crosby hymn "Tell Me the Story of Jesus" was her theme song. "Sweetest that ever was heard!"

....

CHAPTER 12

High School Days

Ecclesiastes 12: 1 "Remember your Creator in the days of your youth, before the days of trouble come and the years approach when you will say 'I find no pleasure in them.'" NIV

DAISY WAS NOW IN high school. The weather was very cold. Tom and Daisy had to get up every morning and build fires in two stoves. That heat felt so good. Mom Kelley made large pans of biscuits from scratch. Breakfasts were big at the Kelley house. There was not much later in the day though. Mom Kelley did not have an easy life. She had the bare necessities but hung on to her faith. There were many times when the family was hungry. Dad Kelley finally went to Welfare to get some raisins, flour, salt and a few basics. He did not like doing that, but did not want to give up drinking.

The bronchial issues Daisy had contracted from the whooping cough were beginning to intensify. She would be so cold and stay behind the old wood burning stove as much as possible. When she told her Dad she was chilled and feverish, he would reply, "Go out in the snow and it will take your fever down." He had no compassion, and never even came close to getting a doctor. While in high school, during a routine student check on health issues, a doctor discovered that Daisy had bronchial problems. Like Paul in the scriptures, this would be her "thorn in the flesh." But God's grace is truly sufficient. Daisy was playing softball on the team and was told to give it up. The doctor recommended that she go into a hospital for a while to be evaluated. This she did but it was a county hospital. It was a long month that she was there. She had to undergo a painful test with no anesthetic. It left her in a trauma. She had a boyfriend, Paul, who came to see her. His mother made her a pair of pajamas. No family member came to see her. A brother-in-law came to take her home. He was the only one who had a car. But Daisy was told that she must either have a drastic surgery or leave for Arizona. She had two weeks to decide. Her folks did not say anything one way or the other, in fact, they showed very little interest at all. Finally, Mom Kelley said: "I don't think you should have that surgery." Daisy was glad to get some response. It was at that moment, that she mentally began to pack her small bag for the trip to Arizona.

In the meantime, she was living with her sister, Henrietta and husband, Ivan. They subsequently had six children: Barbara, Janet, Wanna, Sharon,

Kevin and Larry. She was attending a different high school. She was selected to enter the International Speech Contest. What an exciting event that would be for Daisy. She made straight "A's" and was a cum laude student. But the health issues would get in the way. She told the doctors about this and they said, "You must leave for Arizona." Daisy asked the doctor where in Arizona she must go. The doctor said to go to either Bisbee or Phoenix. Daisy asked him which town was the biggest as she would have to have a job. He told her Phoenix was the larger of the two. Daisy always worked after school and on weekends. She was required to give her Dad half of what she made. With the rest she was to buy her clothes, schoolbooks and shoes. It was not an easy life. She did not get to go to football games, basketball or other fun things. Daisy was not allowed to wear lipstick. One day she appeared in the living room with lipstick on. Her mother told her to take it off until she got out away from home. Her father said it looked like "lip bleeding."

When her sister Margaret, was four years old, she had pneumonia. Dad and Mom Kelley did not call a doctor. Daisy went to the house and saw the gaunt little girl coughing so hard. She finally told her Dad that if he did not take Margaret to the doctor, she would not live. With that statement, Mom Kelley insisted he take her to the doctor. She began to improve very soon afterward. Was this Daisy's turn to save a life? She hoped she had done exactly that.

Leroy married Joan and they had six children: William, Lindale, Troy, Kent, Charlene and Darren. Brother Tom and wife Jean also had six children: Susan, tragically killed in a horse accident at the age of 25, Wayne, Stephen, Tracey, Christopher and Michael. Margaret and husband Joseph had two children: Karen, who died from a blood clot following pneumonia at the age of 41, and Richard. Sister Cora and husband Carl, who has since passed away, had one daughter, Lisa. Brother Melvin and wife Linda had two daughters, Cindy and Gayla.

CHAPTER 13

....

First Date

Hebrews 13:5 "…Never will I leave you; never will I forsake you." NIV

Daisy's first kiss came on the way home from church. Bob had brought her home in his car. Her sister and another fellow were in the front seat. When they reached home, Bob just reached an arm around Daisy and kissed her. Daisy was so shocked that she jumped out of the car and ran to the house. She was very nervous about this first kiss.

A little later on she met Warren and walked through the park with him. He held her hand, a first for Daisy. She was always afraid her Dad would find out. He did not think Daisy should be interested in boys yet. In those days, boys respected girls and did not get aggressive.

Mom Kelley had always warned all the daughters that they must stay pure as the driven snow or no one would ever want to marry them. It was easier in those days as the boys were trained in the same way. During the war, Daisy met other boys, some military, some not. All were respectful and nice.

Daisy seemed to enjoy the boys but was not really enamored of any at the time. But after all she was still very young. This Daisy was still blooming.

CHAPTER 14

War and Remembrance of It

Psalm 25:2 "O my God, I trust in thee: let me not be ashamed, let not mine enemies triumph over me." KJV

LATER ON WHEN WORLD War II started, brothers Leroy, Tom and Melvin all enlisted. Daisy wrote to them and sometimes sent cookies. Leroy fought in Germany and was wounded there. He did receive the Purple Heart. He was sent to a Paris, France hospital, to recuperate. Brother Tom went to Okinawa, and then to London, England, where he built airport runways. It was there that he met his future wife, Jean. They were married in England and then returned to the United States. Brother Melvin served in the Air Force. He had been based in Clinton, OK. He went to Tripoli. He met his future wife, Linda, who worked on the base in Clinton, OK, where they still live to this day. Paul did a short stint in the Navy. Daisy always hoped they would all come home safely.

Daisy had a job at The Belvedere Restaurant. The LST Boats were built on the River in Evansville. The sailors, who worked on the boats, came into the restaurant. Many soldiers came in too during WW II. One day a soldier was sitting alone at a table and Daisy was the waitress. The soldier said he wanted black coffee. This was Daisy's first day and all the coffee she had seen looked brown. She went in to the kitchen, got some coffee grounds and boiled them on the big stove. When it looked black enough, she poured a cup and brought it to the soldier. Then another soldier came and asked another waitress for a cup of black coffee, and Daisy overheard it, so she told the waitress that she had just boiled some in the kitchen. The waitress poured his coffee from the big urn and did not use Daisy's concoction. Daisy was amazed and the waitress told her that the coffee from the urn was what they wanted – just no cream. What a shock for Daisy. The soldier she served that awful stuff to, left her a hefty tip. He realized it was her first day on the job. Many of the military men were drunk when they came in. Daisy's boss told her to serve them tomato juice or black coffee.

The sailors, marines and army men all liked to play the jukebox. They played "God Bless America," "Goodnight Irene," "Always," "I'll Be Seeing You," and "When Johnny Comes Marching Home Again." During this awful time, Daisy missed one soldier, Bill Ferguson, who was killed on Fiji Island.

Tom Brokaw, in his book, "The Greatest Generation." talks about the 2nd World War era and post war time. The one blessing that the United States had then was unity among the people, the like that has not been known since. The people stood shoulder to shoulder, all pulling in the same direction toward peace and "war no more." Tom captures the scene by revealing a list of different people's experiences in the war zone and comments in some way. When the war ended in 1944, after the atom bomb was dropped in Japan, there was joy and jubilation in the streets. The Democrats champion President Roosevelt, who had served three terms, died in April of 1945. Daisy was working in a restaurant when she heard the news of President Roosevelt's death. It was Harry S. Truman who would be in office next. It was his decision to drop the Atom Bomb on Japan, which ended the war much sooner and saved many U.S. military lives.

Daisy was really too young for the job in the restaurant, but she needed the money, so she fibbed about her age. She put her long brown hair up on top of her head to look older. It was here she met Ray, whom she dated for a while. Her grandmother, and her mother, liked Ray. She never wanted Ray to see where she lived or to meet her father. One day, Ray took her home and said he was going to go up to the house to meet her father! Daisy was very horrified about that, but he insisted and pushed right on in. He said: "Mr. Kelley, my name is Ray. I date your daughter." Daisy's father looked surprised but he liked Ray's courage and took to him right away. One day Ray told Daisy that they were going to Chicago and get married. Daisy told him she was not going. Ray explained that he had already gotten permission and the blessing from Dad Kelley. Daisy told him he had forgotten to ask her first. She explained to Ray that she thought she was too young to even be thinking about marriage.

Ray decided he would then date a girl friend of Daisy's. He went into the military and when he came home on leave, Daisy thought he did look handsome in the uniform. He went ahead and took out the other girl but came back and ask Daisy again. He had been trying to make her jealous. But Daisy did not love Ray. She only liked him. Sometimes God says "NO." He closes a door. Daisy was always thankful for all the "NO's." He knows what is best – "...*all things work together for good, to them that love the Lord.*" Rom. 8:28.

Later Daisy met Paul. He went to Central High and she went to Bosse. They had a good friendship but in the end, Daisy had to say no again. Paul gave her a sheathed knife for a going away present when she was ready to leave for Arizona. He told her she would need it because there were only Indians in Arizona. How Daisy dreaded to take that first step off that train. Paul was unhappy when Daisy left. Daisy learned to appreciate the NO answers that God gave her. He was always right. Daisy liked Paul but that was not enough for anything more.

CHAPTER 15

A Leap of Faith into the Unknown

Hebrews 11:1 "Now faith is the substance of things hoped for, the evidence of things not seen." Verse 9-10: By faith he (Abraham) sojourned in the land of promise, as in a strange country, dwelling in tabernacles with Isaac and Jacob, the heirs with him of the same promise." KJV

SINCE THE DOCTORS HAD said that Daisy needed a dry climate like Arizona, Daisy started to get ready for the long trip, this big leap of faith into the unknown. The unknown is scary. But Daisy thought about that night when the man almost abducted her, yet God saved her from that. Would this be any different or worse? She told her mother who thought it a good idea for Daisy to go since it would be better for her health. Daisy told her father and she was surprised at his response. He simply said: "Good luck." Daisy was hoping for a hug instead. She did not feel like she would be missed that much since there were still seven other children at home. Daisy sold her only big possession; a bike. She got $40 for it. Her Aunt Daisy sent her a little money. After she bought the train ticket, she had $60 as her life savings. This she put in the money belt she had been given and tied it around her tiny waist for safety. She was so reluctant to go as she had aspirations at the school, but she had no choice. Daisy was excelling in all subjects at school but she would pursue all that again later.

Packing was easy since she had so little to pack. An older half-sister, Sophia, went to the station with her to see her off. Daisy waved goodbye to the last familiar face she would see for a long time. Sophia, like Hallmark, seemed to care enough to give her very best; she went to the station with her. She was embarking on a "trip to Bountiful." Daisy was seventeen years old and knew no one in Phoenix. God, and God alone, would be with her on this long journey into the unknown. "...My God and I go in the field together, We walk and talk as good friends should and do...He tells me of the years that went before me, When heavenly plans were made for me to be: When all was but a dream of dim reflection; To come to life, earth's verdant glory see...But God and I go on unendingly." Text: Austris Whithol. – Music: Mozart and Whithol.

It was cold on the train, especially at night. A soldier sat beside Daisy and threw his heavy army coat over her. It felt warm and Daisy fell asleep. Soon she felt an arm go around her waist. Sure enough, this soldier was after her money belt!

What else could he possibly want from this frail girl? Her naiveté kept her from thinking he could have any other ideas. Her money belt held her life savings – it was her life line. Daisy jumped up and threw the coat off. She told the soldier she had a knife and asked if he would like to move to another seat. With that, he moved and took his warm coat with him.

Daisy thought about her siblings she left behind. What choice did she have? Daisy was headed for a new place, leaving behind all she had ever known. What would become of her? She would reach forth for the new horizon God would set before her. On the train, Daisy met two girls around her own age of seventeen. They, too, were headed for Phoenix. They had come from Minnesota. One of the girls, Margie, had eczema badly and thought the warmer climate could help. The other girl, Virginia, came along with her for company. Daisy was so alone so she asked them if she could stay close to them just so she would have someone. They consented.

> *Philippians 3:13-14 "…but this one thing I do, forgetting those things which are behind, and reaching forth unto those things which are before, I press toward the mark for the prize of the high calling of God in Christ Jesus." KJV*

"HOW GREAT THOU ART" - Carl Bobero. Second verse: "When thru the woods and forest glades I wander and hear the birds sing sweetly in the trees, When I look down from lofty mountain grandeur and hear the brook and feel the gentle breeze, Then sings my soul, my Savior God, to Thee, How great Thou art…" His power throughout the universe is displayed! Of course, this wonderful God that Daisy knew and trusted would not let a sparrow fall unbeknownst to Him; surely He would watch after this ever blooming Daisy. He would make a way in the desert. Surely this would be a "new thing" for Daisy in a land she had never even heard of or seen before. She would absolutely need the Lord to guide her in this wilderness and show her the way in this desert.

> *Isaiah 43:18,19 "Remember ye not the former things, neither consider the things of old. Behold, I will do a new thing; now it shall spring forth; shall ye not know it? I will even make a way in the wilderness, and rivers in the desert." KJV.*

CHAPTER 16

....

A Place in the Sun for Daisy
Cowboys and Indians

John 15:33 Jesus said, "I have told you these things, so that in me you may have peace. In this world you will have trouble. But take heart! I have overcome the world." NIV.

THE TRAIN ARRIVED IN Phoenix and Daisy stepped up to the door. She was very apprehensive about this step forward. She thought about all those Indians with arrows. Would they take her to an Indian tepee? Would she have to make fry bread? Or worse, would she have to raise little "braves"? Daisy got her knife ready and stepped off the train. She looked all directions quickly, scanning the whole area. She could see no Indians or Cowboys either. She would not be afraid of the cowboys. After all she had seen a Gene Autry movie and they seemed nice mostly. It was a great relief to her not to see what she thought would pose danger. This indeed would be Daisy's place in the sun. This would surely be "blossom time," for Daisy. Here was the sunshine she needed.

Daisy suggested that all three of them get a room in a hotel for the night. She said she would take the cot. The next day they rented rooms in a rooming house. The two girls had a rather large room and Daisy had a small room at the other end of the hall. Daisy asked the girls if she could hide her money belt in their room, since they would be there all day to watch it for her. They said it was OK. So Daisy put the money belt in the sleeve of a sweater and hid it one of their bureau drawers. She thought she had done the best thing possible. She was sure her money would be safe there. She should have put it in a bank.

Daisy went to an employment office and asked for a job. She knew there was no check in the mail for her, and she would have to make her own way. She took the first job offered her. Daisy knew it was God's will that she should work in the health-juice bar. It was a complete health food store. All older women worked there. It was like Daisy had four or five "mothers" now. What a blessing. They had lots of advice and Daisy welcomed their interest. When she started work there, she was ever so skinny. The place served lamb stew and cookies. Daisy could eat the stew and a cookie when she got off work at 4 p.m. It would be enough to last until the next morning. Her God would supply all her needs.

Psalm 84:5-6 "Happy are those who are strong in the Lord. When they walk through the Valley of Weeping, it will become a place of refreshing springs where pools of blessing collect after the rains." NLT

CHAPTER 17

....

Truly "No Cash in the Attic"

Genesis 50:20 "But as for you, you thought evil against me; but God meant it unto good." KJV

DAISY NEVER HEARD ANYONE ask "Who wants to Be a Millionaire?" Instead the very first day when Daisy came home from work, she got a real shock. Her money was gone, belt and all! Daisy was terrified – her life savings gone. She asked the girls about it. Neither one knew what happened to it, they said. A lady across the hall, married to a serviceman, came up with a $60 dollar brooch that evening that she said she had just purchased. That was a little too obvious. Daisy became somewhat of a sleuth and gathered these women all together. She told them that if they would return the money, she would not call the police. It didn't work. No one stepped up to the plate to confess. Daisy knew not to call the police – they would just tell her she should have put it in the bank. Daisy was only seventeen years old, very naïve, and often half sick with fever. She had trusted these new found "friends." One of them took the money. They were at home all day. No one else knew it was there. Daisy never would know who took her money. Virginia got a job, but Margie never did. Her folks sent her money. This left Daisy with a lot of suspicions. "Who Done It?"

Fortunately, Daisy had $12 in her purse to sustain her until payday. She had paid the rent. She bought a large box of Ritz Crackers and they became her mainstay for several months. Some days she didn't feel like eating. The girls did talk her into going to a restaurant and though she was not hungry, they told her to order a plate lunch and eat at least some of it. Daisy did that and it helped her gain some strength back. Getting out in the early dawn to catch a bus was hard on her. It was cold and she did not have adequate clothing. Daisy never once thought to ask for welfare help or any other. She just kept plugging away at life. "One Day at a Time – Sweet Jesus, That's all I'm asking of you."

The first thing Daisy did when she arrived in Phoenix was to find a church. She had to find one she could walk to since she had no car. She joined First Southern Baptist Church, never realizing that her future husband was watching that day. The church was a real blessing to her, and she met some friends in a Sunday School Class. God was still watching over this young girl who was so far away from home. She was still smiling through her difficulties. She missed her Mom and siblings. But Daisy was blooming – one petal at a time. To add to her blessings, the couple who owned the rooming house asked the girls to join them for dinner on Thanksgiving. It was the first home cooked meal Daisy had eaten since she left Indiana in October.

Thanksgiving People

T   hanks giving people give thanks to God,

H   is grace is shed on all –

A   re you a thanks giving person

N   ot forgetting sometimes to recall,

K   indnesses, sweet friends, and trees,

S   ongs, pretty birds, and love;

G   iven freely just for us and it

I   s bestowed from Him above.

V   ery special we are to Him

I   n all our wont and erring ways,

N   ot once does He forsake and Thanks-

G   iving people share the praise!

—Dee

....

The first Christmas was not easy and Daisy's mother sent her a small package. Mom Kelley did not know how to package things and it arrived all broken. The small bottle of perfume had spilled onto the stationary. But Daisy did not care about that. At least her mother had tried and had thought of her. Her boyfriend sent her a dress. Fortunately, Daisy had naturally curly hair and did not need beauty shops that she could not afford anyway. Because of that, she could be ready for holidays quickly.

One of the ladies at the juice bar, Mrs. Coffee, wanted Daisy to meet her wonderful nephew, Philip. He seemed very nice. He asked Daisy to take a plane ride with him. He owned a small plane. Daisy had never been on a plane and it sounded like fun. After all he was Mrs. Coffee's nephew. So she went with Philip and boarded the small plane. Up, up, and away they went over the city. What a fun ride this would be. After a short while, Philip came upon what looked like a field of corn or wheat he seemed to know. It could have been a cotton field. There was a bare strip of land in the middle of it and Philip brought the plane down there! Daisy became very frightened! This was not a good situation. Philip grabbed hold of Daisy and pulled her to him. He kissed her hard, causing her to cry. Suddenly he was advancing to some inappropriate moves! Daisy cried out to him and warned him of what would be the result of his actions. She told him to stop and get hold of himself. When he continued advancing, Daisy said, "I wonder what your Aunt Ethel would say about this." She told him she was only seventeen years old. With that he stopped. He got back in the pilot seat and took off for home. Daisy left him as quickly as possible.

Two days later Philip came to her door asking to talk with her. Daisy rebuffed him but he insisted. He wanted to take her out to dinner to prove that he really was sorry for his actions. He was afraid Daisy might tell Aunt Ethel. Daisy told him she would never get in to a vehicle with him. He said there was a fine restaurant within walking distance. Finally, after much pleading, Daisy consented to go only if they walked. So they did. They had a lovely dinner and walked home. Philip never touched her. He apologized over and over. Daisy never told Ethel Coffee about her adventure with Philip.

The rent for the room was $10 a week. It took most of Daisy's paycheck to pay it. She had to have bus fare and food. The owner of the place told her that if she would take a room mate her rent would only be $5 a week. Daisy agreed and the owner sent a woman. The woman moved in, but Daisy sensed that this was an experienced woman. She had a strangeness about her. In one corner of the room she had a stash of weird nuts, seeds, etc. that she ate. She said she posed for pictures for a living. She asked Daisy if she'd like to do the same. Daisy suspected that she posed in the nude. The first night she went to bed nude. Daisy shot up upon this discovery and told her she could not sleep nude in her bed. Daisy had long flannels on herself. The next day, Daisy asked her to leave, explaining that they were not at all compatible. A man came to pick her up. They told Daisy that she was like a thirteen-year-old girl – not mature. That did not bother Daisy – good riddance. She would just pay more rent.

Would Daisy be able to survive in the desert? Her soul mate – the Lord – was there to guide her through the murky spots. It took some time for her to connect at the church and make some friends. The women where she worked were friends but of a different age group. It was always so amazing to Daisy how God took her small, immature hand and led her forward.

CHAPTER 18

Daisy Gets Married

Psalm 34:3 "O magnify the Lord with me, and let us exalt his name together. KJV

FOR ENTERTAINMENT, THE TWO girls and Daisy decided they would go to a dance. Daisy had not learned much about dancing but she would try it. Dancing was a no-no at home. It was at this dance that a young handsome man came and asked Daisy to dance. She was reluctant at first, looking him over with her "Eye of the Day" look. She had not liked what she had seen there for the most part. After a scrutinizing, she decided to dance with him. Later, he called her and they went out. His name was Duke, and he worked for the Southern Pacific Railroad. His brother came along on their first date, mostly because it was raining and Duke had no car.

In the spring of the following year, Daisy saw an ad in the paper for another room in a different location. She went to see it and it was better for her. Mrs. Campbell owned this home. It was a private home. At first Daisy had a small room in the basement with another girl, but the girl moved and Daisy moved upstairs to a nicer room of her own. Mrs. Campbell played the piano and did not mind for Daisy to pick out some right hand notes of hymns. It was a better place for sure. Daisy was moving on up, it seemed. Daisy tried to re-enter school but found that she did not have the strength to work and go to school. That would come later and it did. Daisy finished school a few years later.

Ephesians 5:17 "Wherefore be ye not unwise, but understanding what the will of the Lord is." KJV.

But Daisy continued to date Duke and he was a nice man. He was the youngest in a family of eight children. Daisy was still working and riding the bus to and from work. By June of that year, Duke and Daisy were married by Rev. Vaughn Rock of the First Southern Baptist Church. But before they married, she wrote to Paul and told him of the pending marriage. It was Paul's mother who responded to Aunt Daisy. Of course, the news came on to Daisy of Paul's request to be sent far away. He was sent to Japan. Daisy had never wanted to hurt him.

John 12:34 "A new commandment I give you, that ye love one another; as I have loved you, that ye also love one another." KJV

CHAPTER 19

Bible Baptist Church

Psalm 55:22 "Cast thy burden upon the Lord, and he shall sustain thee: he shall never suffer the righteous to be moved." KJV

THE CHURCH WAS THE center of the family's life. It was at this juncture, Daisy rededicated her life to the Lord. She wanted to be of more service to Him. In the church, she taught an eighth grade Sunday School Class which proved to be quite a challenge. She worked with the women's ministry. Also she served as a deaconess which involved helping with baptisms, communion cups, etc. Her husband sang in the choir and also did solo work. He had a beautiful tenor voice.

After Daisy and Duke's son, Duke Lamont, nicknamed Monty, was born, they decided to build a house. They did so without a loan and it took them four years to literally build it by hand, brick by brick. They both worked at regular jobs during the day and built on the house at night and every weekend. Brother Leroy came and helped pour the cement floor. They used a "story line" to lay the blocks. They and a neighbor friend had made the blocks themselves. Then the foundation had to be poured. ("How Firm a Foundation." – "K"---in Rippon's Selection of Hymns, 1787). Daisy and Duke knew they needed a firm foundation in life as well as in the house. That foundation in life was their Lord, Jesus Christ. Daisy was out mixing cement and pouring it in the foundation. The pastor of the church they attended, Reverend Petznick, came and saw her doing work that he considered too hard for a small woman. He told her she was going to injure her health and should not continue to do that, but wait for the men to do it. Pastor Petznick, and the members of Bible Baptist Church, a Conservative Baptist Church, decided to get a gang together to come and help put the roof on the garage where Daisy, Duke and Monty were living while waiting to build the actual big house. Daisy baked pies to serve with coffee for the helpers. In a day the members had the job done. They lived in the temporary quarters for four years, while working frantically to get the house built. It was finished enough to move in to just two months prior to daughter Gina Lynn's birth. Daisy remembers being down on her back at seven months pregnant putting a sink in the kitchen. She learned to put in plumbing, put up plywood where needed, put on wallboard, and put in firebreaks. They did not do the electrical work. It was a glorious day when they finally could move in to the big house. ("O Happy Day that fixed my choice On Thee, my Savior and my God...Happy Day, when Jesus washed my sins away." Haldor Lillenas, 1885-1959). After the house was finished, together they built a duplex apartment on the back lot. The hardest job was holding up a 26-foot-long two-by-six board on the eave of the apartment. Daisy was up on a ladder for that one. The apartment helped with income but was a lot of work and worry.

Daisy went to help out on the building of the apartment. While she was out, Gina, asleep on the couch when Daisy left, woke up, climbed up to the medicine cabinet and got the baby aspirin. She ate a whole small bottle. When Daisy came back in a short time later, Gina said she had taken the pills for a headache. What an alarming situation that was. She was immediately taken to the hospital where they had to pump her stomach. The doctor said he did not know how things would turn out; it depended on how long the pills were down. They took her home and held her tight. Neighbors came in. It was a most scary time. For many hours, the hospital and doctor kept calling to see how she was. Finally, Gina said: "I want an ice cream cone." One neighbor ran to get a cone and another got the ice cream which Gina ate heartily. The doctor called again and Mom and Dad told him that good news. He said she was going to make it alright from then on. He said to give her anything she wanted and, of course, they jumped to get it. Gina was three years old. Daisy never bought another baby aspirin again. God had rescued them and their precious daughter ("Rescue the Perishing." Fanny Crosby, 1820-1915). They had done a lot of praying.

One day Daisy did a foolish thing. Monty had been asking to drive the car. He was a mere child. But Daisy thought she would let him back the car up a little just to please him. He was only eight years old. He got in and Daisy ran along the side holding on to the car. But Monty pushed hard on the accelerator and nearly pinned Daisy against the block wall belonging to the neighbors. Daisy was yelling at Monty to get his foot off the pedal which he did. But the wall was knocked down. Daisy and Duke spent the night rebuilding the wall. It was a fool thing to do and Daisy should have known better! After they got the wall built back up to snuff, they all went down to Hamburger Inn and got a hamburger to celebrate. Daisy learned a hard lesson on that one. She told Monty to ask again to drive when he was twenty-one! She also learned the answer is "NO" sometimes.

Early in their marriage, there were some problems. They tried to work around them. Daisy so wanted to keep the marriage in tact. Things got better for some time. Daisy so wanted to have her family – that was utmost to her. Five years later, little Terri Sue came into the family. What a wonderful life, Daisy thought. Pastor Petznick came to see their child and said she was beautiful! She was.

Daisy quit her job and stayed home for the next nine years and concentrated on raising her children. She cooked and cleaned and the family did simple things together, like playing games. The family took a vacation every summer. They went to Duke's childhood home in Arkansas first. This was a large country home with wide porches and big oak trees. It was like Tara, the O'Hara home, in *Gone With The Wind.* A person could even have a swing in one of those huge trees. This was such a homey place.

Daisy loved Duke's mother whom everyone called Mama. Papa had been a school teacher and was somehow connected to the cotton gin to work. Duke's sister, Theara, was always there and she was very nice to Daisy. Mama and the girls cooked fresh vegetables from their garden every day. Daisy especially liked the summer squash. The family was large and many came in the summer. Another sister, Armenta, was a special one to Daisy. She had two children, Jackie and Jerry Jones. At present, Jerry Jones is the owner of the Dallas Cowboys. They were all so nice to Daisy and she loved their visits on the front porch. The only bad thing was the outhouse was out through the pasture. Sometimes Daisy would get stuck there waiting for cattle to pass on by as she was afraid of them.

THE HOUSE OUT BACK – "The house out back, I remember well; As I recall those days gone before – The house out back had a half moon on the door. Those trips could be cold in rain, sleet or even fog, But one thing for sure, there was a Montgomery Ward catalog." Ah, sweet memories!

The Arkansas farm was a place of canning fruits and vegetables, bathing in a number three galvanized tub, churning real butter, and corn bread made on top of the stove. What a delightful place. It was truly like a southern plantation.

From Arkansas the family traveled on to Indiana. ("Back Home Again in Indiana"). Daisy loved visiting her folks there and usually stayed at her brother, Tom's. This again was a large family and always involved a family picnic. Besides all the good food, they played the "washers" game. This is an Indiana game and the family never missed an opportunity to play. Even Daisy's parents took part in that. Mom Kelley especially loved to play and some of her throws could be rather wild. When she did get a ringer, she would jump for joy. To this day the family still gathers and plays the washer game.

For lack of funds, Daisy and Duke would have to cook along the road on these trips. It did not matter as they were young, the children were young, and all had energy. They made any sacrifice to go. It was always a renewal time.

> *Psalm 51:10 "Create in me a clean heart, O God; and renew a right spirit within me." KJV*

CHAPTER 20

....

Surgery

Isaiah 26:3 "Thou wilt keep him in perfect peace, whose mind is stayed on thee; because he trusteth in thee." KJV.

Psalm 31:24 "Be of good courage, and he shall strengthen your heart, all ye that hope in the Lord." KJV.

WHEN TERRI WAS TWO years old, Daisy had to have the long awaited lung surgery. It was so very serious. Yet the Lord sustained her even through that surgery. Daisy's husband was very helpful during this time. Daisy never would forget. On the fourth day after the surgery, Daisy sank to a low point. The nurses summoned the doctor and also her pastor. Pastor Petznick came even though he was half shaven. He prayed for Daisy. Daisy remembers the doctor: Dr. Mellick, who said: "get the tubes out of her nose – she does not like anything in her nose." Soon Daisy began to make progress. Pastor Petznick was a true saint. He cared so much. All around Daisy were those who cared. Her children were a great comfort to her during that time.

Yes, there were happy times. The family went for rides, went to get a root beer, or ice cream. Daisy loved having her family all around her. There was that perfect peace many times over.

Daisy went to visit a friend who was working in the school district. She had Terri in her arms then. Gina was in school and Monty too. The administrator there asked Daisy to go to work there for a short time while someone was out sick. Daisy consented. She worked there for the next two-and-one-half years.

Later Daisy went to work for the Phoenix Union School District. She and her husband came to a fork in the road. He took one fork and Daisy took the other. They parted after 20 years of marriage. This was a sad time for sure. There was no animosity between them and they remained friends throughout life.

After that Daisy had her share of loneliness, mistakes, and some difficulties getting by financially. Also getting up in the middle of the night to irrigate was a hassle and a scary one. The yard was large and there were fruit and shade trees to be watered. But in the end she saw Romans 8:28 come to fore: "All things work together for good to those who love the Lord, and are the called according to His purpose." Daisy always trusted that the Lord knew best even though she got some "NO" answers along the way. Yes, and they were always for her good.

CHAPTER 21

Getting on with Life

Isaiah 42:16 "I will turn darkness into light before them and make the rough places smooth." NIV.

DAISY WOULD NEED THAT lamp unto her feet in the darkness spoken of in the scriptures. She would need the rough places smoothed out for her as only her Savior could do. She needed Him every hour.

Daisy learned to deer hunt. She would be loaded down with gear, guns and whistles. She would lie down beside a log and watch. Once she saw a deer come out in front of her but soon saw it was a doe. It was such fun just to hunt for them. Mearn's quail came out in her sight and they were so beautiful. Daisy was fascinated by this mother and her fluffy yellow little ones following her. That was a memorable sight in the Tucson Mountains. Daisy loved the outdoors and seeing wild animals – at a distance, of course.

It was during this time Daisy learned to play golf. She did well at it and thought it good exercise.

She played with several friends from work. Most of the time she came out on top, but that was never the main point or even mentioned. Daisy loved the game and the fellowship. She learned the golfer's hymn, "There is a Green Hill Far Away." This was something she could and would do the rest of her life for as long as possible.

Daisy did community work and enjoyed it. This was part of a professional growth program in the school district where she was working. It was necessary to have community services as well as college credits to apply for salary increases.

Daisy was alone with her girls for the next thirteen years, and son, Monty, was off to Vietnam. When he returned and was married, he pursued a Master's Degree in Business Administration. There were lots of lonely days and nights. Daisy was not saying a lot, but her thoughts were deep. Prayer was constant. Her focus was on guiding her teenage daughters. She would surely need God to make the rough places smooth down a lot of rough roads.

Daisy always thought it was a difficult decision at times to know which way to go - to burn your bridges or go ahead and cross them. She would need a lot of guidance on this one.

CHAPTER 22

....

The Bicentennial Trip –
and Beyond

Psalm 119:105 "Your word is a lamp to my feet and a light for my path." NIV

DURING THIS TIME, IN 1976 – the bicentennial of our Country – Daisy took the girls and a friend of Terri, Linda, on a very long trip all the way to Cape Cod. She drove a 1971 Monte Carlo that she kept in good condition. The trip was exciting. The first real stop was in Arkansas where the girl's grandmother and aunts lived. When they arrived, Daisy stayed in the car and let the girls go in. But Duke was there at the time and came and got Daisy and ask her to please come in. She did and was received with open arms. Mama came from a back room to see Daisy. By this time Mama was about 100 years old. She lived to be 106 years old. She hugged Daisy and said she was so glad to see her. The girls' Aunt Theara was there too. She was always such a sweet person. She was a retired school teacher. They had a wonderful visit and then Daisy and the girls loaded in the car and left for Indiana.

There they had a great visit with Daisy's family. Her mother was 74 by now; her father had died in 1950 at the age of 63. Mom Kelley was right when she said alcohol would cut his life short. Mom Kelley had never even thought of remarrying, though she was only 48 at the time of his death. She was left with six children to rear alone. What a tremendous job was ahead of her.

After that, they headed on to Cape Cod. They visited Gina's intended husband's family in Dennis, MA. They had a very pleasant time on the Cape. Daisy was so pleased with these three girls. Each day one would pay for meals and gasoline. They would jump out and wipe the windshield and pump the gas. They were so congenial. Daisy believed they really did enjoy the trip. From the Cape they headed for Niagara Falls. What a sight that was. They went to the Canadian side first.

By the time they all reached home, they had traveled over 6,000 miles. It was a milestone, unforgettable trip that proved to be educational as well. It was one of those sweet spots in their lives.

The girls and Daisy kept busy. They were in school and Daisy was working in the school district. She felt that she had the best bosses ever. The last one was Mr. Scott. He was a gem and they worked together well. On Saturdays, Daisy would start cleaning in her far north bedroom and the girls would start in their far east bedrooms. They would work their way toward the middle – the kitchen. Then they would have lunch. The girls were involved in gymnastics, track and just seeing friends. Lots of their friends came to their home. There were sleep-overs, games, and other fun activities. Daisy loved having them there.

Daisy liked the name of Gina Lynn; it fit this blue-eyed, pretty girl. She received an AA degree in Art and had studied art all through high school and college. Her oil, water colors, clothing, jewelry, lampshades and murals were all outstanding works. She always loved horses from the time she was small. From a petite girl, she grew into a pair of cowgirl boots. She went into the business of boarding horses, massaging horses, holds a therapy certificate, and she teaches horseback riding. Gina modeled shoes, took bit parts in movies, and represented Mary Kay products, just to name a few of her many involvements. She was commissioned to paint the mural on the wall at a northern Arizona ski lodge. Gina taught art as well. Most recently, she wrote and published the book, THE SECRET BARN DOOR. Her second book has been published and she is working on her third one.

In the year 1977, Gina married Dick Beck. They had two girls, Lyndsay Marie and Summer Dawn. Daisy loved them and enjoyed them every possible chance. However, Dick was a pilot and therefore he was gone a lot. This made it hard for Gina as she was alone too much. She always had to carry most of the load at home. Gina worked hard with the horse business, and in other areas.

Terri Sue, the youngest petal, had a pediatrician named Dr. Terry. He was so kind to both mother and child that Daisy decided to name her Terri because of that doctor. Terri had graduated from high school in 1978. She, like her sister, has many talents and accomplishments. She has a special knack for decorating, remodeling, and making a yard to envy. Yard art got to be a real specialty for her. She was never afraid to be adventurous with color. She could turn most anything into something beautiful. Terri liked painting walls, pictures, and other forms of art. Terri was also a very creative cook. Her husband, Steve, provided a great "honey-doer" for her. Terri and Steve have enjoyed their dogs: Sox, Jessie, Co E Bear, and Bonnie. The dogs stay well behaved, clean, and spoiled. Terri also has a knack for giving her mother the right cards with lots of thought, as did her brother and sister. Both Terri and Gina seem to be blessed with many talents. Monty had special talents too in a different way.

CHAPTER 23

Vietnam for Monty

Luke 1:74-75 "That he would grant unto us, that we being delivered out of the hand of our enemies might serve Him without fear, In holiness and righteousness before Him, all the days of our life." KJV

IT WAS DURING THIS time that Monty went to Texas and enlisted in the military. He had finished up at Arizona State University and went to Officer's Candidate School in Virginia. When he graduated, Daisy and the girls went to pin the bars on him. The ceremony there in Fort Belvoir, VA was so impressive. While there, they toured Washington, D.C. visiting the mint and all the monuments. They also visited Arlington Cemetery along the Potomac. It turned out to be quite educational. Monty went to the School saluting officers, went to the ceremony still saluting, but when he came out, the men were saluting him. Daisy was so very proud of him.

Then Monty shipped out to Vietnam. Daisy spent the next year praying for his safe return. When he came home, Daisy had a huge sign made

– WELCOME HOME, MONTY! This they put up across the whole front of the house. What a relief it was to have him home safe and sound. This was another answer to prayer. ("God Will Take Care of You.")

When Monty returned after his stint in Vietnam, it was not too long before he married the girl of his dreams, Mary. They met in a church in Houston. They were married in 1972. They had two sons, David Alexander and Douglas Lamont, who subsequently had families of their own. This was always a very close-knit happy family.

WE HONOR YOU

"Our young friends—yes, young friends, for in our hearts you will always be young, full of the love that is youth, love of life, love of joy, love of country—you fought for your country and for its safety and for the freedom of others with strength and courage. We love you for it. We honor you. And we have faith that as He does all His sacred children the Lord will bless you and keep you; the Lord will make His face to shine upon you and give you peace, now and forever more."

....

1988 Speech – Remarks at the Veterans Day Ceremony at the Vietnam Veteran's Memorial on November 11, 1988 by Ronald Reagan - 40th President of the USA

CHAPTER 24

·····································

A Surprise Visitor

Acts 2:46-47 "Day after day they met as a group in the Temple, and they had their meals together in their homes, eating with glad and humble hearts, praising God, and enjoying the good will of all the people." TEV

As DAISY CAME HOME and pulled into the driveway, she thought she saw a figure in the dark yard. She entered the back door and did not turn on lights. She peeked out the backdoor window and sure enough the dark figure was coming toward the door! Frightened beyond imagination, Daisy ran to a back bedroom to grab a phone. By that time, the man was banging on the back door. Daisy managed to call the police who tried to keep her on the line. She kept telling them the man was banging on first the back door and then the front door, so please hurry. When he hit the front door Daisy ran for the back door. Then he was banging on the back door. Daisy thought she would try to run out the front door but just about that time she heard his voice: "Mother, mom, mom, it's me, Monty."

Daisy opened the door and the two of them clung to each other. Daisy was so relieved to find it was her son. He had come home through the back yard. Together they decided they should celebrate this wonderful ending by making a big sundae. They were laughing about the crazy set of circumstances, and eating the sundae when all of a sudden, lights were everywhere – all over the carport and the house. The police were knocking on the door. Daisy was so embarrassed as she had forgotten she had called them. She opened the door and explained to the officer that it was her son. He told her not to feel bad at all. He said that just two blocks away a man had broken in to a home and the lady was not so fortunate. He assured Daisy that she had done the right thing by calling. Once again, God had put his angels around Daisy and her son. It reminded her of Jeremiah 29:11: *"For I know the plans I have for you," says the Lord, "They are plans for good and not for disaster, to give you a future and hope." NLT.*

A similar incident happened another dark night. Daisy's neighbor, Ray, had come to her home to see about the irrigation which turned on in the middle of the night. He had no flashlight and all Daisy could see was a man on the carport. She called the police who came and demanded some identification from Ray who had none. They came to Daisy's door and ask if she knew the man. Daisy told them that he was her neighbor and all was well. Once again, Daisy was ashamed that she had called the police but was assured again that it was the right thing to do.

Living alone had its bad points. Daisy was scared. She had a Derringer hand gun. Some nights when she would hear noises in the other end of the big house, she would get the gun, cock it, and go searching through the house one room at a time, one closet at a time, until she was satisfied that no one was there. She put a heavy nightstand up against her bedroom door each night. She really thought this was no way to live happily ever after. One would think her faith had waned since she feared for her safety. She trusted the Lord though really to watch after her (sometimes not her fellowman). ("My Faith Looks Up to Thee." – Ray Palmer, 1808-1887) Daisy was grateful that she never had to fire the gun.

It was about this time that Daisy was dubbed "DEE." She liked it and it stuck. 1987.

CHAPTER 25

Daisies Sometimes Tell!

Daisy Belle, Daisy Belle,
Is my real name,
No claim to fortune,
No claim to fame.

It may seem strange,
Maybe even sort of crazy,
My friends call me "Dee,"
But my real name is Daisy.

Now I've never liked "Daisy"
And vowed I'd never tell;
What if my name was Tinker,
My middle name is Belle.

Though I've never liked "Daisy,"
Didn't want to be a "Rose,"
My mother liked "Clementine,"
But "Daisy" won by a nose!

The Blooming of a Daisy

In my youth I was "Daisy Mae,"
Charmed by "Lil Abner,"
In my teens I was "Daisy June,"
Red Skelton tried to nab her.

Through all that I finally
Emerged as just a "Dee,"
So whatever you call me,
I just gotta be "ME."

I should be ever grateful,
And just sit back and hum,
What if my dear mother
Had liked a chrysanthemum!

I'm only known as "Daisy"
By doctors, lawyers, and such,
But friends, please call me "Dee"
If you want to stay in touch!

By Daisy (Dee)
March 27, 1987

....

DURING THE TIME WHEN Daisy was single and the girls were grown and married, Daisy went back to Indiana each summer. She and her sister, Margaret went on five-day trips to Kentucky, Ohio, northern Indiana, or sometimes Tennessee. They just wanted to get away and share, bond, love, and play cards. They ate at some interesting places, or went to a flower show, such as Ameriflora in Ohio, or whatever sounded interesting. Those were very precious times for both sisters. They continued these trips for many years even after Daisy was married as she went back in the summers. Daisy thought it was all still a part of blooming time.

CHAPTER 26

....

A Life-Changing Decision

Another Petal Blooming

Romans 8:38,39 " Neither death, nor life...nor anything else in all creation, will be able to separate us from the love of God in Christ Jesus our Lord." NRSV

AFTER THE GIRLS WERE married and left home, Daisy, who had become Dee, was indeed in the empty nest. The house was big and lonely. During these lonely years, Dee dated a few men. Nothing clicked. She continued to attend church, which was Grace Community Church. Fridays were the hardest for her. At work, people in her office would tell of all they were going to do that weekend – going to the mountains, to the ocean, to the movies with their mates always. Dee felt most lonely when she heard this as she was going home to a lonely house. Ruth Graham, daughter of Ruth and Billy Graham, wrote a book titled IN EVERY PEW IS A BRO-KEN HEART and Dee could really relate to Ruth. One

Friday night in September, 1986, Dee went into the room in the back of the house. It was a large room. She had her television, radio, and even a tray to eat on. She was doing some cleaning and listening to a minister on the radio. He said: "Seek ye first the kingdom of God and His righteousness, and all the other things will be added unto you." Matthew 6:33. All of a sudden it hit Dee: FIRST – Had she put Him first? Had she let anything come between her and the Savior? Had she fully put her whole trust in Him FIRST? There was that word again looming up in her mind. Dee knelt beside the bed and prayed for the next hour asking Jesus to become like new to her and remind her once again that she needed to put Him first. She prayed for guidance for the days to come. She let go and let God. And did He take hold of her anew! Dee had never left out going to church, praying, and giving. But this was a GRACE AWAKENING, loud and clear. The blooming of this Daisy (Dee) was well under way. (Sanctification.)

Dee slept that night and got up with a smile. The depression was lifted. She did not even feel lonely. The Lord shut some doors and opened up some others. She quit dating altogether. None were going anywhere anyway. She took classes at church. She started doing more writing. At work she wrote the school newsletter. Then she went to a square dance and wrote a newsletter for them. Also she was involved in a Christian Singles Class and wrote a newsletter for them. She loved creative writing. She enrolled in college. That was mostly for professional growth through an incentive program. But she loved it and she was far too busy to be lonely. She led orientation meetings for Parents Without Partners, also a part of the incentive program. She saw her children every chance possible. She joined Scottsdale's Toastmistress Club. She learned that every "er... er," cost a dime! Life took on new meaning. God is so good. ("Praise Him, Praise Him, Jesus our blessed Redeemer..." – Fanny Crosby, 1820-1915). This Daisy was still blooming!

CHAPTER 27

This Time of My Life

The time has come in my life when
I can wear purple and rose,
I can order what I want to eat,
I'm even allowed to doze.

I don't have to clean my plate,
Or hoe and plant those seeds,
I don't have to clean the house today
And I don't have to pull those weeds.

Life for me is set in family,
And love for all my friends,
My Lord supplies all my needs,
I just keep up with loose ends.

The weeds of life need pulling,
Then maybe sprigs of love will show,
When sprinkled then with kindness,
The daisies begin to grow.

There will come a day ere very long
When we'll see Jesus face to face.
What a day that will be for us,
We'll recognize His Amazing Grace!

Written by Dee – Year 2002

....

Psalm 90:12: "Teach us to realize the brevity of life,
so that we may grow in wisdom." NLT.

CHAPTER 28

....

That Man on the Mountain

*Jeremiah 6:16 "Stand at the crossroads and look;
ask for the ancient paths, ask where the good way is
and walk in it and you will find rest for your souls."
NIV.*

THAT NIGHT DEE HAD prayed that God would either
make her useful and happy as a single person or
bring only a Christian man into her life. God did
both. For the next six months, Dee was a happy
single keeping very busy and thankful that she was
able to do what she did. Men were out of her life,
and she was not thinking about meeting anyone
special. But God's plan was about to unfold even
more. A friend, whom Dee had not heard from in
about six or seven years, called her. Zelda had met
a man in the Sunday School Class named Casey.
They had married and were very happy. Casey
had a brother-in-law from Montana who had lost
his wife some time back. Zelda at first ask Dee how
her love life was: Dee told her it was anywhere between zilch and none. They visited a while and

nothing was said about anyone else. Several days later, Zelda called again. This time she asked Dee if she would like to meet a Christian man from Montana. Dee knew that Zelda was a true born again Christian herself and would not introduce her to a dud. With that in mind, she said "yes." Zelda and Casey came with Bill to Dee's house and picked her up to go eat out. When Bill told Dee his last name, Dee thought she would never want to marry anyone with such a complicated name as Van Egmond. Yet there was something about this man that was different. He was a gentleman, a Christian man, and seemed to like Dee. He asked Dee for a date.

Dee planned the day and took Bill on the Apache Trail. They stopped along the way to look at the beautiful scenery. There was a place in the mountains called Tortilla Flats. They stopped there where Dee's former Sunday School teacher and his wife worked. Charles and Ethel met Bill and enjoyed a long talk over what they called Killer Chili. After the visit, Dee and Bill moved on up the trail. They came across a whole herd of deer, and saw elk too, on the road. It was a beautiful "Sentimental Journey," to be sure. They had another wonderful connection. Dee wondered if Bill was sent from God: after all, she had asked God to send a Christian man if she was to meet someone. Later she knew that Bill was sent from God. Bill knew that Dee got a Spring Break for about a week. He called and asked if he could send Dee a ticket to

Montana. He said he wanted her to meet his family. This Dee did even though she was a little nervous about it. She was amazed at the place where Bill lived. There truly were purple mountain majesties all around. There were the Bridgers, the Tobacco Roots and other ranges of mountains all around. The ranch was considered a small one by Montana standards, but seemed huge to Dee. She met the family including Bill's sisters and brothers and his nieces and nephews. This was a large family.

Dee was anxious for Bill to meet her family as well. Everyone seemed so congenial. Bill flew back to Phoenix on a visit. Then came summer and Dee made another visit to Montana. It was obvious that this was a forever connection. Dee was about to make a phone call to her son when Bill asked her to wait a minute. Then he proposed to Dee in such a tender way. This was indeed a sweet spot in their lives. Dee and Bill were married later that year at Soldier's Chapel in Big Sky, Montana. That was a joyful, happy September day.

("Whither Thou Goest" – Guy Singer) "Whither thou goest I will go, Wherever thou lodgest I will lodge." This was there wedding song.

("LOVE LIFTED ME." - James Rowe) "When nothing else could help, Love Lifted Me."

Colossians 3:17 "And whatsoever ye do in word or deed, do all in the name of the Lord Jesus, giving thanks to God and the Father by him." KJV

CHAPTER 29

....

The Indiana Hoosier
Club of Arizona

*Mark 3:35 "For whosoever shall do the will of God,
the same is my brother, and my sister, and mother."*
KJV

DEE LATER WAS THE founder of the INDIANA HOO-
SIER'S CLUB OF ARIZONA in 1985. She started with
only a few comers. But the club grew to around 200
solid Hoosiers. It was enjoyable. Dee led the group
and had some entertainment, but always included
prayer. There would be a meal and then recogni-
tion of new people. Most of the people came from
the northern part of the State. Dee used to tease
them by saying the reason was that it was so cold
up there they had to come south.

Dee paid for the expenses of printing flyers,
renting places to meet, and other necessary things.
Finally, one day one of the first members, Charles
Pell, a Ball State graduate, told Dee that others
would like to share in the expense of running the

Club. After that, each one paid a $1 to come. No one objected and it helped a lot toward expenses. Dee led the Club for 10 years before she finally gave it up. There were no takers for her job and so the club disbanded.

After Dee and Bill were married, Bill helped her with the Club. He enjoyed visiting with the people. It was a fun project and made for many connections. Dee regretted that no one would take up the job and carry forth. It was time consuming and no one had that much time to spare.

CHAPTER 30

····································

Home on the Range

Psalm 50:10 "For every beast of the forest is mine, and the cattle upon a thousand hills." KJV

DEE AND BILL LIVED on his ranch in Montana in the summer months. The other six months they spent in Arizona. They enjoyed both places. In Montana, Dee wanted to have the experience of raising some cattle. They bought some Charolais and kept getting more all the time. Dee became proficient as a helper in the cattle business. She learned that ranching and farming is a real science. No more milk stools and churns. They went to cattle sales and bought what they considered cows genetically worthy. They were a challenge to raise. Dee was afraid of some of them, especially the bulls. Dee helped with the shots (Dee "chuted" them and Bill "shot" them) and spraying of the cattle, as well as the record keeping for these registered cows and bulls. She did not know how many head (why not tails, same number) they had. Cattle language at times could be "udderly" ridiculous, but Dee learned a lot. One of their Charolais cows and her bull calf made the cover of the National & International Charolais Journal. It was all in the genes. They did have a couple of "bum steers" and they had to go to market. Dee even learned how straw is made. She wondered, does everyone know how straw is made? The cows all had names like Miss Perfect Choice, Miss Mac-a-damia, and Miss Special D. But the first cow they bought they named Miss Dee Light. She proved to be just that and was very productive. Their main bull (sire) was named Big Sky Sly. He had the high genetics.

Life on the ranch was new to Dee and everything about it was different. It was great with many highs and a few "lows." If was not only from the cattle, but also with other woes. But all in all Dee was happy. God was so good, and life was joyful. At one time or another, Dee's children came to Montana to visit. Many friends came too. They were excited and amazed at all that went on. Gina went on a trip to Ovando on a horse ride into the Bob Marshall Wilderness. She did see a grizzly in there, but said it was a fun trip. Bill and Dee went to Ovando to see her and stayed at a quaint old hotel there, The Blackfoot Inn.

They rode 4-wheelers around the ranch and kept a close watch on the cattle. Dee crocheted several afghans, made three quilts, and made straw wreaths. The quilts were a Sunbonnet Sue & Suspender Sam, a Colorwash Irish Chain, and a Bird-house quilt. Bill made her a very unique quilt rack from a set of elk horns. There was not another like it in the world. It was exciting to create something new. Isaiah 43:19 *"Behold, I will do a new thing; now it shall spring forth..." KJV.*

Dee and Bill went on a cruise to the Panama Canal, two trips to Hawaii, and a trip to Ireland, England and Wales. These trips were with friends and that made them even more special. They loved going fishing in Montana and in Canada.

The Franklin Graham Crusade went to Boze-man. Many lives were turned around there. Bill and Dee worked as volunteers in the Crusade. The man who trained the volunteers was from Ireland. One night over 300 high school and college- age students responded to the call. It was a powerful Crusade.

In the winter time the Van Egmonds lived in Phoenix, Arizona where they had a home in the mountain area surrounding Phoenix. They attend-ed church in both places. More petals were bloom-ing on this Daisy. It got so hot in Phoenix, that they liked escaping to Montana in the summer.

And Dee put it this way: IT'S TOO HOT!

CHAPTER 31

It's Too Hot!

It's too hot. The temperatures soar
To one hundred and eight and more.
My shoes are off; I'm in the shade.
I'm drinking quarts of lemonade.

It's too hot to work, too hot to play.
I find I'm sweating most all day.
I'm wearing thin clothes on my back,
And my skin is dry and about to crack.

The AC is working hard to cool my bones,
All I want are big ice cream cones.
We'll go somewhere cool for a while,
But we come back in winter with a smile.

When the "dry" heat's gone and the weather's great,
It's a joy to be here; no one hundred and eight.
Yes, it's too hot in the middle of summer,
To miss the winter, would be a real bummer!

Thank God for the heat; it reminds us of Hell,
It's a real place, don't live in a shell,
Seek the Lord while He may be found,
Let God in your heart, and be heaven bound.
By Dee – 2007

CHAPTER 32

Wonderful Experiences with XYZ

(extra Years of Zest)

*Job 23:10 "But he knows the way that I take; when
he has tested me, I will come forth as gold." NIV.*

DEE KNEW THAT SHE was still in the refining process,
and she also knew God would be with her all the
time. Dee had the wonderful privilege of being
asked to emcee a program for, XYZ the senior group
at Grace Community Church; the program was
themed "HE KEEPS ME SINGING." Dee chose Psalm
96 to share. She had the great honor of introduc-
ing the world famous special speaker and hymn
writer, John W. Peterson. He wrote hymns such
as: *HEAVEN CAME DOWN, IT TOOK A MIRACLE, OVER
THE SUNSET MOUNTAINS, SO SEND I YOU, SPRINGS OF
LIVING WATER, SURELY GOODNESS AND MERCY and JE-
SUS IS COMING AGAIN.* He had composed over 1100
individual songs and over 34 cantatas. The cantatas include *NIGHT OF MIRACLES, BORN A KING, NO
GREATER LOVE, CAROL OF CHRISTMAS, EASTER SONG,*

JESUS IS COMING and *DOWN FROM HIS GLORY*. There were well over eight million copies of these cantatas published and sold. Mr Peterson is a member of the Gospel Music Hall of Fame and is listed in Who's Who in America as well as in the world! Dee thought Mr. Peterson was such a gracious man and ever so humble. What a wonderful privilege to be selected to make his introduction.

Dee also had the privilege in XYZ of telling about the life of Bill and Gloria Gaither. That was another glorious day to tell about this wonderful couple. They too had written many hymns such as: *THE OLD RUGGED CROSS MADE THE DIFFERENCE, GOD GAVE THE SONG, HE TOUCHED ME, BECAUSE HE LIVES, THE KING IS COMING, SOMETHING BEAUTIFUL and THERE'S SOMETHING ABOUT THAT NAME* just to name a few. Bill Gaither said: "Christian music isn't just a style, it's a theology wrapped up in a lot of different styles; it's the message that unifies us. Gospel music is a beautiful message." Bill Gaither was inducted into the Gospel Music Hall of Fame in 1983. Bill and Gloria Gaither said they hoped their southern gospel music would "bring the warmth of His love to your soul. May they be a message of refreshment to lift our spirits." Dee loved southern gospel music. It was her joy to study the history of the Gaithers and to be able to tell the assembly about them.

Dee enjoyed modeling clothes for XYZ along with other friends. One such program was titled

"SECOND HAND ROSE." These were fun times. Also Bill and Dee put together a program called "DOG-PATCH U.S.A." – "COUNTRY "HAY DAY." They even brought in bales of hay to put on the stage and decorated that with pitchforks, spades, quilts and mop dolls. During the summer, Dee made fruit jars full of Montana wheat, and decorated them with cloth for table centerpieces. Inside she put a recipe for wheat salad. A number was drawn so that one person at each table took that home with them. It was a lot of work, Dee recalls, but it was worth the time.

CHAPTER 33

··

A Montana Welcome to XYZ

1 Corinthians 13:13 "But now faith, hope, love, abide these three; but the greatest of these is love." NASB

BILL AND DEE WELCOMED a bus load of XYZ seniors to Montana and hoped it would be a delightful stay for them. The theme was Hawaiian and it was held at the Holiday Inn in Bozeman. Of course, they sang "Home on the Range." Then Dee gave them her version of the song:

I got me a home
Where the buffalo roam,
Where my family and I play,
Where often is heard
A discouraging word
Like why didn't you dehorn some today!

And often at night,
The bulls start to fight,
And I'm getting my ranch education,
I stand there amazed
And asked as I gazed –
What is this artificial insemination?

The cattle are grazing,
It's just so amazing,
This Home on the Range is for me.
The calves are a nursing,
They don't need rehearsing.
Welcome to the folks from Grace's XYZ!

....

The evening was blessed by a group of eight men called THE HIGH COUNTRY MESSENGERS. One of them was a nephew, Al Bos. Bill & Dee asked the group to try to pick out the nephew. They missed and picked another man. They felt that the whole bus load had a great time in Montana.

Bill and Dee enjoyed many trips and programs with the XYZ group. Dee enjoyed doing a lot of em-cee work, leading prayers and leading the program on the day the leaders of the group retired, Helen and Arnie File. Dee wrote a tribute to them. Dee featured all kinds of ships in her tribute beginning with LEADERSHIP. FRIENDSHIP was next, followed by MEMBERSHIP, COMPANIONSHIP, RELATIONSHIP AND STEWARDSHIP all describing Helen and Arnie. Their favorite songs are: Helen: "Ivory Palaces" and Arnie's "When He was on the Cross." Dee felt sure God would say to them "Well done, good and faithful servants." Fortunately, Paul and Dottie Hartzler took over as leaders of XYZ and they have done a marvelous job. Personally, when times got tough, they were great hands- on helpers and encouragers. Praise the Lord for saints like these.

Dee also led a program for the same group on THE BEAUTY OF A WOMAN. This followed the life of Esther of the Old Testament. Esther was such a woman of determination even to the point of risking her life. She said "…If I perish, I perish." What a courageous woman she was, and she was willing to lay down her life for her people. Psalm 139:14 "…*I am fearfully and wonderfully made…*" *KJV*

Erma Bombeck put it this way IF I HAD MY LIFE TO LIVE OVER – April 21, 2000 – "I would have burned the pink candle sculpted like a rose before it melted in storage." She said "Don't sweat the small stuff…Let's think about what God HAS blessed us with."

"Sweeter as the Years Go By." - Lelia N. Morris, 1862-1929. – "Richer, fuller, deeper, Jesus' love is sweeter, Sweeter as the years go by."

....

CHAPTER 34

Live Your Someday

DEE AND BILL ENJOYED almost 13 years of married life together. Then God took Bill home to Glory. His very last words were to Dee – "I love you." ("Love Lifted Me." James Rowe.) And indeed it did.

The Lord watched over Dee closely the next few years. Though they were lonely, there was more blooming to do. And God opened another door! Another petal was forming. Bill's sister, Irene, was an angel sent from God to Dee after Bill's home going. They took trips around Montana and just enjoyed life. Others too, stepped in and were such a comfort. It was time to just *Be still and know that I am God." Psalm 46:10. KJV.*

Dee saw a sign on a large billboard that read "Live Your Someday." This was Dee's "Someday." To put it another way, Jonathan Swift said: "May you live all the days of your life."

The Blooming of a Daisy would go on as there were more books to read, more books to write, more service for Him, more love to give, more songs to sing, and most of all, more great grandchildren to enjoy. Three and one-half years later, Dee was married to David S. Price whom she met at the church they both attended. They attend IN-Joy!, a senior group at Arizona Community Church. This group is led by Pete and Sandy Peterson and they do a great job. They took over for Martha and Wes Pierce who gave them a super example to follow. Dee and David attend XYZ as often as possible. God put just the right people in just the right places, at just the right times. Dee should not have been surprised at that. Yes, the Blooming is still going forward. Praise His Holy Name.

> *Psalm 91:1,2 "Those who live in the shelter of the Most High will find rest in the shadow of the Almighty. This I declare about the Lord; He alone is my refuge, my place of safety, he is my God, and I trust him.." NLT.*

> *Philippians 4:8 "And now, dear brothers and sisters, let me say one more thing as I close this letter. Fix your thoughts on what is true, and honorable, and right. Think about things that are pure, and lovely, and admirable. Think about things that are excellent and worthy of praise." NLT.*

CHAPTER 35

Christians and Steaks

Dee B. Van Egmond
Manhattan, Montana

Christians and steaks – a strange combination,
For lots of reasons – there is a relation,
And sometimes both come under condemnation.

Christians and steaks are sometimes tough;
Some are thick, some are thin and very rough,
Of Christians and steaks, there are not enough.

There are lean ones and those that are fat,
Big ones, small ones – some fly off the bat;
Of Christians and steaks, some seem like old hat.

There are brown ones, red ones and some are black,
Crusty ones, burnt ones and some you must hack,
Bony ones too, not enough meat even to attack.

Christians and steaks- some are so tender,
But sometimes both go back to the sender,
Plus all that, they come in either gender.

Christians and steaks – what about the rare one,
Others dried up like they were cooked in the sun;
Then there are the ones that are really well-done!

Christian and steaks – both a real delight;
If perfectly prepared, they make you feel alright,
And both come from God – what a beautiful sight.

Christians and steaks – make you think of a steer,
Some are real pilots and seem very dear,
And some are so good, you need have no fear.

Of Christians and steaks, this is no bull;
Some you have to push and others you pull,
If they're no good you are soon so full.

Christians and steaks seem so much the same;
But only the Christians have Christ in their name,
Still we remember from whence they both came.

So in life we must look out for the fakes,
Since it can be in both, the Christians and steaks!
So watch for the real ones for goodness sakes!

Yes, steaks are so good – what joy they impart,
But only the Christian has God in his heart.
So Christians and steaks right here must part.

So you see it is here the similarity ends,
And this analogy and the message it sends,
Because Christians and steaks are just good friends.

....

Published in the 1993 anniversary edition of
The Montana Poet Magazine

120

SUMMARY

Dee has always known that other people have had similar circumstances growing up. She feels that it should never be a reason, or excuse, not to climb higher, set achievable goals, and work toward them. One can look back at history and see how many successful "greats" are out there who had less than the best while growing up. Not all who were born with the silver spoon reach success in life; in fact, many go the opposite direction. God has given people bright moments to look back on. Dee had, since childhood, a "yearn to learn." She has a curious mind and wants to understand why things happen as they do. The book focuses on several main points: her near abduction, the 1937 flood that destroyed their home, and her lonely transition at the age of seventeen from Indiana to Arizona. Dee says be thankful for the times when you sat on Daddy's lap, got good grades in school, when you were rescued from the storms of life, that you had an "Aunt Daisy" to pray for you, for a mother's teachings and warnings, or when some-one did something so nice for you with no hope of repayment. Psalm 139:14 says *"You are fearfully and wonderfully made."* Each one has gifts and special talents to be offered to God and each one should brighten their corners every chance they get. Philippians 4:8: *"...If there be anything of good report, think on these things."* We should think about things that are excellent and worthy of praise.

Throughout the book Dee has referenced appropriate hymns and their authors. Dee loves the old hymns and believes the true message is in them.

Dee feels so blessed that God gave her a great family, many friends and the joy of being around to enjoy them. God is so good. It is Dee's hope that possibly something in this book, *"THE BLOOMING OF A DAISY,"* will be an encouragement to many to rise above negative circumstances through God's marvelous grace. Dee knows that when the Lord calls her home, she will have reached full bloom. Until then, she will keep blooming, one petal at a time. In the pursuit of happiness we need a strong hope, a strong faith in God, love for others, and a strong finish. "There are only two ways to live your life. One is as though nothing is a miracle. The other is as though everything is a miracle." – from HeartQuotes: Quotes of the heart – Albert Einstein. Growing up, Daisy had a lot of miracles. But after all: Romans 8:31 says: *"What shall we then say to these things? If God be for us, who can be against us?"* KJV.

Pastor Charles R. Swindoll is one of Dee's very

favorite writers. He is so forthright and clear. "The person who succeeds is not the one who holds back, fearing failure, not the one who never fails— but rather the one who moves on in spite of failure. Move forward–trust God." Charles R. Swindoll, Taken from Insight for Living 2003 calendar, "Adventuring With God." (Used by permission.) May God bless you as you enjoy the "Sweet Spots" in life.

ABOUT THE AUTHOR

Dee (Daisy) B. Van Egmond-Price makes her home in Phoenix, Arizona. She is retired from the Phoenix Union High School District where she worked for twenty-one years. Dee spends her time with her husband, children, grandchildren and now great grandchildren as much as possible. She is a member of Arizona Community Church, IN-Joy! Seniors, and XYZ Seniors. She and her husband, David S. Price, volunteer for various services, both in church and in an assisted living facility. Dee loves to make chili and does weekly. They are involved in the Gideon International ministry as well. They love to play golf when the weather is nice which is most of the time in Arizona. Their favorite golf course is Rolling Hills. They like to travel by car to many places, most recently to Florida on a "Gospel Tour" to visit many churches, most of which they watch on television. They were most impressed with Pensacola Christian College. While on this trip they visited sister, Cora. They made another long sad trip recently to Indiana, Dee's birth state, to attend the funeral of a dear forty-one-year old niece, Karen.

Dee likes to write. She writes a personal monthly titled newsletter with distribution to between 70-100 relatives and friends. She has written poetry throughout her adulthood. Dee's life scripture is Matthew 6:33: *"But seek ye first the kingdom of God, and his righteousness; and all these things shall be added unto you."* KJV.

Mission statement: Dee wants to live an exemplary Christ-like life, always seeking His will. She prays for each member of her family daily. Her greatest desire is that they all know Jesus as their personal Savior and that they would walk with Him daily. She knows then that they would "rejoice with joy unspeakable and full of glory" as spoken of in 1 Peter 1:8. She would like to use her God given talents, whatever they may be, to glorify God and to make a difference in this old world. Dee believes that one can rise above their childhood circumstances and move on with His divine help.

"CHRISTIANS AND STEAKS" - by Dee B. Van Egmond was published in the May, 1993 issue of *Montana Poet Magazine.*

Printed in the United States
200324BV00001B/430-528/A